DEEP MINISTRY IN A SHALLOW WORLD

NOT-SO-SECRET FINDINGS ABOUT YOUTH MINISTRY

CHAP CLARK & KARA E. POWELL
From the Center for Youth and Family Ministry

ZONDERVAN®

Youth Specialties
.com

ZONDERVAN.com/
AUTHORTRACKER
follow your favorite authors

Youth Specialties

Deep Ministry in a Shallow World: Not-So-Secret Findings about Youth Ministry
Copyright © 2006 by Chap Clark & Kara Powell

Youth Specialties products, 300 South Pierce Street, El Cajon, CA 92020 are published by Zondervan, 5300 Patterson Avenue Southeast, Grand Rapids, MI 49530.

Library of Congress Cataloging-in-Publication Data

Clark, Chap, 1954–
  Deep ministry in a shallow world : not-so-secret findings about youth
ministry / Chap Clark and Kara Powell.
     p. cm.
  ISBN-10: 0-310-26707-2 (pbk.)
  ISBN-13: 978-0-310-26707-2 (pbk.)
  1. Church work with youth. I. Powell, Kara Eckmann, 1970– II. Title.
  BV4447.C512 2006
  259'.23—dc22

                                                                2006004005

Web site addresses listed in this book were current at the time of publication. Please contact Youth Specialties via e-mail (YS@YouthSpecialties.com) to report URLs that are no longer operational and replacement URLs if available.

Creative Team: Dave Urbanski, Doug Davidson, Janie Wilkerson, Laura Gross, and Mark Novelli
IMAGO MEDIA
Cover design by Holly Sharp
Printed in the United States

06 07 08 09 10 • 12 11 10 9 8 7 6 5 4 3

ACKNOWLEDGMENTS

The well-known African proverb reminds us, "It takes a village to raise a child." We know that's true for children, and we think it's true for books, too.

Thanks to our executive committee at the Center for Youth and Family Ministry for supporting this book and helping it take shape.

Thanks to Paul Shrier, Andy Root, Ron Hammer, Bill Dyrness, Juan Martinez, Mark Lau Branson, Rick Beaton, and Tod Bolsinger for your ideas about how the academic discipline of practical theology can be both appealing and accessible for youth workers.

Thanks to Matt Westbrook, Brad Griffin, Cheryl Crawford, Mark Maines, Jason Djang, and Pam King for your willingness to read part or all of the manuscript. Your fingerprints are all over this final product.

A special thank you (and a great big hug) from Kara to Dave, as well as to Nathan and Krista, for your willingness to allow this book to become part of our family's mission and ministry for the last nine months. Dave, your gentle strength makes me a deeper lover of Jesus and others. Nathan and Krista, I'm grateful for your patience when I had to place writing ahead of playing with soccer balls and Play-Doh. I'm even more grateful for those times when you knew I needed a break and dragged me to the living room to read a book or see your "new tricks."

And thanks, too, from Chap to Dee, Katie, Rob, and Chap. You guys continue to teach me what it means to follow Jesus with depth, passion, and integrity.

And lastly, thanks to our colleagues and students at Fuller Theological Seminary. We cannot imagine a more integrated, warm, and dedicated community of scholar-practitioners who are committed to "deep ministry in a shallow world." Your partnership in life and ministry has made this book possible.

"Backed by solid theological reflection and heartfelt experience, Chap Clark and Kara Powell invite all of us who care about kids to discover creative, natural, and inspired forms of youth ministry that have the power to cultivate a lasting faith."

Mark Yaconelli, Author of *Contemplative Youth Ministry*

"Kara Powell and Chap Clark have presented an engaging project for those who care about the church and young people. In this text they push us away from our too-often-used consumer mentality of youth ministry ("tell me what will work") and toward a reflective process (about ourselves, young people, God's action). The authors also present a new paradigm called "deep design" which paints a picture of how one can do ministry at deeper levels, moving the youth worker from being a church programmer into being a reflective practitioner. This book will be of value to all youth workers who read it."

Andrew Root, assistant professor of youth and family ministry, Luther Seminary, St. Paul, MN

CONTENTS

SECTION 3: DEEPER PRACTICES

CHAPTER 8
Deep Communication: Why Doesn't Our Teaching Change Kids' Lives?
Chap Clark

CHAPTER 9
Deep Missions: Why Are So Few Kids Interested in Service and Missions?
Kara Powell

CHAPTER 10
Deep Worship: Who Are Students Becoming When We Lead Them in Worship?
Kara Powell and Brad Griffin

CHAPTER 11
Deep Expectations: Why Am I Exhausted So Much of the Time,
and What Can I Do about It?
Kara Powell

CHAPTER 12
Deep Focus Groups: In the Midst of the Busyness and Crazy Expectations,
How Can We Maintain Deep Ministry?
Kara Powell

SECTION 1
A DEEPER PROCESS

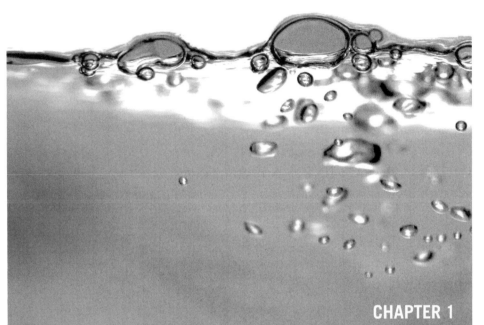

CHAPTER 1

WHAT KEEPS US FLOUNDERING IN THE SHALLOW END?

Chap Clark and Kara Powell

WHEN KARA MET JANA

I remember the day I realized our ministry was splashing around in the shallow end. It was 10 years ago, and it was all because of a student I'll call Jana.

Jana was a party girl. From sleeping around to spending most of the weekend drunk to her daily hits of marijuana, Jana did it all. That is, until she let Jesus take over her life.

As soon as Jana got involved in our ministry, I was drawn to her. It was one of those "God-type" connections that I couldn't ignore. Since I was trying to develop a student leadership team, I asked her to meet with me every other Tuesday after school. Every time we met, sometime between 4 and 4:30, she'd ask me what time it was. (Still a bit of a free spirit, she never wore a watch.) I'd tell her, and then we'd go on with our conversation.

After her fourth Tuesday doing this, I asked her why she cared so much about the time. She answered, "Oh, it's not really about the time. It's about my old habits. I used to get high every afternoon at 4:20. Now that I'm into Jesus, I like to know when it's 4:20, so I can think about how different my life is now."

Not exactly your typical "church kid" answer, eh?

A few months after Jana and I started meeting, our ministry launched a Sunday-morning series on sharing our faith. When our teaching team was brainstorming potential guest speakers, I thought immediately of a couple at our church whose evangelism ministry focused on sliding Jesus into conversations whenever possible. Since I wanted our students to know how to talk with their friends about Jesus, I asked this couple to teach a few Sundays.

I thought the couple did a great job of helping students see that no matter what they're talking about with friends—from homework to their latest fight with their parents—they could somehow shift any conversation toward Jesus. The goal was to ask non-Christians the right questions, slip in the importance of prayer, and ideally share a testimony whenever possible. We even role-played so students could practice steering conversations toward Jesus.

Watch out campuses, here we come.

The next Tuesday Jana burst my bubble. After we had picked up our frappuccinos, she asked me what I thought about the last few Sundays. I smiled and answered, "Actually, I think we're learning great stuff about how to talk to our friends about Jesus."

She looked down at her straw, clearly unsure if she should share her opinion. I wanted to make it easy for her, so I asked, "How about you? What do you think?"

She looked directly at me. "To be honest, I think we're missing the point. We're making it seem like our friends are projects we conquer instead of people we care about. I didn't decide to follow Jesus because of a great conversation or transition question. I decided to follow him because of how people who knew him loved me. Anything else feels manipulative and cheap."

Was Jana right? Maybe that kind of conversation-twisting evangelism had worked before, but was it too shallow now?

I invited Jana and eight other new Christian kids to my house for tacos. I wanted to find out what had drawn them to Jesus. For all but one, it was the way they saw Jesus' love in his followers.

No keen transition phrases. No subtly sneaking, "I'll be praying for you" into the conversation. Just relationships, 1 Corinthians 13-style.

As I talked further with Jana and other students, I started to question the depth of more than just our evangelism strategy. Was my teaching helping kids see the relevance of Scripture, or was I getting lost in the details of finding the right video clips and telling the right funny stories? Were our worship times enveloping kids in God's love and power, or had they become performances by our most talented musicians? Were our small groups encouraging life transformation, or had they degenerated into weekly times for sharing about science projects and sick pets?

Maybe the shallowness of our ministry at the time was one reason I was working such long hours. My (often unsuccessful) efforts to meet the endless needs of kids and families were robbing me of the downtime I craved—leaving me absolutely empty.

Maybe our lack of depth also explained why my sense of purpose was evaporating. Sure, God had called me to this ministry—but when kids I've invested in keep walking away from him, what's the point?

SHALLOW OR DEEP?

Is your ministry producing the deep change it's "supposed to"? If not, maybe you find yourself losing your sense of balance and purpose, as I did. Or perhaps you're losing other things. Like your sense of compassion. You've done your best to counsel hurting kids, but when they don't seem to get better, you start becoming numb to their pain.

Maybe your ministry's shallowness is taking away your sense of hope. Your church kids aren't all that engaged. Even when they show up, the "do something we

haven't seen before" looks on their faces make you wonder if they'll ever change.

When we aren't seeing deep results, we may turn to Scripture for assurance. After all, Isaiah 55:11 reminds us that God's Word won't return void. As long as we're faithfully sprinkling its seeds around the soil of teenagers' lives, surely some of it will grow deep roots and bear fruit. An apple here, a berry there—it all adds up to something meaningful, right?

Yes, God works in ways beyond what we could ever imagine. Of course his Word is powerful and can take root in kids' lives either through or despite our best efforts. But all good farmers evaluate the state of their crops—and if they're being choked by weeds or drowned by floods, farmers don't comfort themselves by remembering previous bountiful crops. They don't find consolation by pointing to a few healthy plants scattered among acres of scraggly weeds. They roll up their sleeves, investigate new tools, and develop fresh strategies to produce better harvests. They know that if their crops aren't healthy, the end is near.

The same is true for youth ministry. Yes, God is the Ultimate Worker—but if we human workers sense our ministries are shallow, we need to admit that and make some changes. Let's be honest with ourselves and with one another: It's time for deep ministry in a shallow world.

SHALLOW "SOLUTIONS"

It would be nice if we could download into our PDAs God's perfect recipe for a deeper youth ministry. But God rarely gives us such explicit directions. Although we often get some general sense of leading as we spend time with him, God usually allows us to come up with the specifics.

There are three common "solutions" many youth workers impose when they begin to realize their ministries aren't as deep as they'd like them to be. While each seems promising at first, they all end up merely scraping the surface of the problem.

Solution 1: "More of the Same"

When we want to go deeper but don't know how, we often try doing *more of the same*—more of whatever it is we've always done. Often that means more of the same activities. If one overnighter didn't really cut it, then two will do the trick. Small groups on Sundays aren't clicking, but that's because the students don't know one another all that well. If they also met on Tuesday nights, then we could move past pseudo-community and into real-life relationships.

But maybe it's not more activities we need. Perhaps it's more adult leaders. Right now we have one adult for every eight kids. Our adults feel stretched, and our kids don't feel cared for. If we could recruit more adult leaders, then we'd have more personalized time with kids, and that means deeper ministry.

But having more adult leaders and more activities is going to cost more money. Our budget is much smaller than the children's ministry, and don't even get us started comparing the youth budget with the church's worship service budget. If we only had more cash, then we could offer more programs and sponsor more trips—and then God could work more deeply.

Is it so terrible to offer more activities? Not always.

Is it wrong to want a bigger budget so we can offer more programs at cheaper prices? Not necessarily.

Is it so bad to recruit more adults to care for kids? Not at all.

So what's the problem?

There are several reasons we can't just keep mindlessly repeating more of the same year after year and expect our ministries to grow deeper:

1. *Our culture changes.* Whether you're located in center-city Philadelphia, a rural town outside Sioux City, or a suburb of Seattle, you live in an ever-changing culture. Socio-economic and racial dynamics make our cities and towns greenhouses of growth and change. The rapid expansion of the Internet and other information technologies connects communities and individuals across the globe. A rapidly changing culture demands ministries that are able to grow and adapt.

2. *Our theology—our thinking about God—changes.* Although some assert that God changes, we disagree. God's attributes are permanent. They cannot be gained or lost. Of course God can and does interact with us and respond to us and our prayers, but his core qualities remain unchanged.

   So if God doesn't change, why would our theology change? Quite simply because our understanding of God changes. If you're able to read this page, you probably have a light nearby. Imagine that the light represents God. If you put down this book, get out of your chair, and stand on the other side of the room, you'll see different parts of the light stand, bulb, and lampshade. Now, has the light changed? Not at all. Your perspective and understanding of the light has changed. Similarly, God, the ultimate light, never changes, but as we follow God and study the Scriptures, we experience and understand more of his revelation.

As our theology matures, so do our ministry programs. For instance, when we start thinking about church more deeply, we might decide to restructure our small groups. As our beliefs about evangelism expand, we'll train students differently in how to reach out to their friends (somewhere I hear Jana saying, "You know it!").

3. *Our churches change* (admittedly, some change *way* more slowly than others). A church is a community of believers, and as the people change, so will the church. Whether it's because a new leader with different dreams joins the community or because God plants new dreams in existing leaders, as the vision of your church changes, your ministry will, too.

4. *You change.* God continues to teach you, stretch you, and form you. As God develops you, so your ministry should develop. Kara unpacks it further: *One area in which God has most taught me is my desire to look like I have it all together. I've always wanted to give perfect talks, offer flawless advice, and steer our ministry to run seamlessly. But over the last decade, God has helped me realize there's only one Savior, and I'm not him. I've slowly realized that it's not my perfection that ministers; it's my daily sense of being messed up and needing God's grace that does the trick. And the deeper life God has breathed in me in turn breathes deeper life into our ministry.*

Solution 2: "It Worked for My Friend"

When more of the same fails to take us deeper, the second solution is *what's worked for a friend*. We've heard from Mary Robin at the church down the street that service opportunities at the local soup kitchen are working for her kids, so we try it, too. We talk to a college buddy whose

  **DEEP MINISTRY**

kids love the new way they're adding art into worship time, so we rush out to buy our own chalk and clay.

Maybe serving soup and drawing pictures are exactly what our students need. But maybe not. We haven't been to our friends' churches, and they haven't been to ours. We haven't talked to their kids, and they haven't talked to ours. Maybe our situations are so different that what works somewhere else will flop in our neck of the woods.

Plus if we're honest, who among us, when talking to other youth workers, hasn't exaggerated to some degree the depth we're seeing in our ministries? At a conference, you might tell someone your small groups are going "great," but actually they're stumbling along because you don't have enough leaders. You may talk in glowing terms about your new narrative style of teaching, even though parents are telling you their kids don't always get what you're teaching. It could be that what we're hearing from others is what they'd *like* to believe is happening in their ministries, instead of what's really happening.

Solution 3: "That's What the Book Said"

Another attempted escape from the shallow end is following *what the books say*. We just have to buy the latest, hottest youth ministry book and follow its 10 practical steps in our own ministries, and we, too, will see deeper ministry results. (Almost sounds like a blurb from a back cover, doesn't it?) We end up believing we can simply cut and paste the experts' ideas into our own ministries.

Two youth ministry models that have attracted great attention in the last 15 years are the seeker-oriented model of Willow Creek Community Church near Chicago and "Purpose Driven Youth Ministry" from Saddleback Community Church in Southern California. If you read materials from Willow Creek or Saddleback carefully, you'll

Context = a particular setting

Let's be honest: we need a deeper vision for ministry as well as practices that are clear, creative, and compelling. But not just any type of new vision and practice—if our vision and actions don't match God's vision, it's time to dry off and go home. But when our plans embody God's vision, and the new depth brings about the changes that God intends, then we're definitely swimming in the right direction.

note that they stress that what works for them might not work for you. You need to understand the needs and resources of your own ministry before you implement their programs.

Unfortunately, youth workers hungry for immediate depth often skip these well-intentioned disclaimers. We take ideas from Willow Creek and Saddleback, drop them into our own ministries, and expect to double or triple our groups instantly. That might happen occasionally, but youth workers often end up disappointed when their groups don't change overnight.

In the last few years the theology and philosophy embodied by emerging churches has gained significant attention. Many "emergent" leaders, aware that others are looking for a cut-and-paste approach to ministry, avoid giving program ideas. They talk mostly about theology and only hint about methodology. That should avoid the cut-and-paste problem, right?

Not exactly. Many youth workers still grab for whatever programmatic scraps they can find at the emerging church table. They darken the room, light some candles, and use incense, because those are pretty easy changes to make. One trip to the hip coffeehouse in town, and they're set. But they haven't grasped the deep source of tradition that underlies and informs these practices. It's a new version of cut and paste called "grab and slap." It means you grab what you can and slap it on top of what you're already doing. Ministry as always—plus candles.

WHAT WE NEED: NEW IDEAS THAT TAKE US DEEPER

Once we realize our ministries are shallow, it's tempting to jump onto ships carrying more of what we've always

done, what's worked for our friends, or what we've heard the experts say. From a distance, these three solutions seem like they might work. But when we take them out for a cruise, we find that our boats start taking on water.

This book invites us all to something deeper. Whether you're a rookie or a seasoned veteran; whether you're a staff person or a volunteer; whether you live in a suburban, rural, or urban context; whether you're feeling disgusted with the Same Old Stuff or just a little discouraged—it's time for a major change in how we think about youth ministry.

WHY DID WE WRITE THIS BOOK?

Simple: to help you come up with a deeper design for your ministry. The two of us have roles at Fuller Seminary that allow us to jump into the ministry pool and learn from other theologians and leaders. In Chap's case, he's an associate professor in youth, family, and culture as well as the director of Fuller's doctorate of ministry program in youth and family ministry. Kara is also part of the faculty at Fuller Seminary, but she spends most of her time serving as the executive director of the Center for Youth and Family Ministry (CYFM). The mission of CYFM is to provide youth and family workers with resources and training that are practical, accessible, and grounded in research—stuff just like this book, actually!

To find out more about CYFM resources that cover the topics in this book and beyond, or to check out our FREE (yes, free!) "CYFM E-Journal," go to www. cyfm.net.

Through our research and resources, we're trying to bridge the canyon between the academic world and the youth ministry world so these camps can learn from each other. This book is our invitation to you to join us in deepening youth ministry processes and practices.

But this book can't draw an exact plan for you. We know youth ministry pretty well, but we don't know *your* youth ministry. We know kids and families, but we don't know *your* kids and families. This book won't give you a perfect-fit plan, but it will help you draw a plan that fits *your* kids, families, and communities. That and only that will capture the shape, color, and depth of your own ministry pool. After all, you're the expert in your context.

We've included application questions at the end of each chapter. They're geared to help you navigate your ministry currents and tides. Use them—by yourself, with a friend, or with your whole ministry team—to think about how the ideas in this book can be most effective in your unique situation.

So toss aside those flotation devices and come with us as we prepare to plunge into deeper waters!

Application Questions:

1. Do you agree that insanity is "doing the same thing over and over again and expecting different results"? When have you fallen into this trap? Why is it tempting to do the same thing over and over again?

DEEP MINISTRY

2. Have you ever felt as though your usual ministry ideas and practices were getting shallow? If so, how did you come to realize this? What did you do about it?

3. Which solution are you most likely to try: more of the same, what works for your friends, or what the experts say? When has this tendency been helpful? When has it not been helpful?

4. How do you feel about learning new, deeper ideas? What makes you nervous about it? What appeals to you?

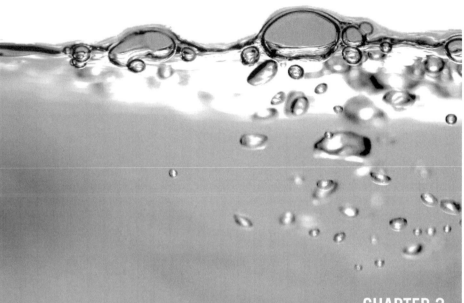

CHAPTER 2

DEEP METHOD: WHAT'S OUR PLAN FOR GOING DEEPER?

Chap Clark and Kara Powell

At the top of my long list of favorite quotes from *The Divine Conspiracy*, Dallas Willard writes, "But now let us try a subversive thought. Suppose our failures occur, not in spite of what we are doing, but precisely because of it."[1]

If our goal is deeper youth ministry, we need a whole new way of doing ministry. This, in turn, means we need a whole new way of thinking about ministry. This new path out of the shallow end has to be pretty special because of all we're trying to balance:

- We want thorough, deep reflection…but nothing too complicated.

- We want specifics…but room for creativity.

- We want it to be practical…but more than the usual Youth Ministry Tips and Tricks.

- We want sensitivity to our own unique contexts… but to still learn from other ministries.

If all that isn't tricky enough, we ultimately want our ministries to be all that Jesus wants them to be.

Yowza.

DEEP DESIGN: AN OVERVIEW

This book revolves around a four-step process we call Deep Design. It's a continually moving and evolving template for ministry growth and change completely tailored to your needs because the issues of your particular ministry define and shape the process and make it work.

Let's unpack it further.

By "discern" we mean "understand."

Step 1 provides the opportunity to discern God's transforming activity in your ministry. Step 2 has you reflect

[1]Dallas Willard, *The Divine Conspiracy* (San Francisco: Harper Collins, 1998), 40.

24 DEEP MINISTRY

upon fresh insights from Scripture, historical thinkers, current research, and experience as you consider what's happening in your ministry. Step 3 invites you to observe others who are integrating these new insights into their own settings and compare them with your situation. Step 4 completes the cycle by helping you apply findings from Steps 2 and 3. As your ministry grows and changes, you will flow naturally from Step 4 back to 1.

To simplify this process, we've developed one over-arching question for each step:

- Step 1 (Discernment): *Now?*

- Step 2 (Reflection): *New?*

- Step 3 (Observation): *Who?*

- Step 4 (Application): *How?*

For those of you who like visual aids (probably most of us), we've created a diagram of the Deep Design process that we'll walk through and add to throughout this chapter.

STEP 1: NOW?   **STEP 3: WHO?**

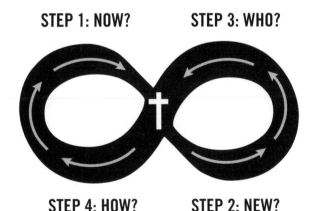

STEP 4: HOW?   **STEP 2: NEW?**

The left half of the diagram represents Our Ministries—both as they are **Now**, and **How** we'd like to see them deepen. While it's tempting to jump immediately from realizing there's a problem to implementing a solution, the reality is that we won't get to choose from the maximum array of solutions unless we engage with the right half of the diagram, Others' Insights, which includes considering **New** information available and carefully observing those **Who** are making use of innovative strategies. The flow of the four steps helps develop the correct balance between looking in the mirror and looking out the window, so to speak.

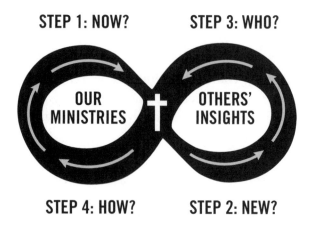

A Caveat: It Will Be Messy

In this chapter, we'll present the Deep Design process step by step, question by question. But you'll find that the actual process isn't always clean, neat, or linear. In fact, it never is.

But we think it's helpful to understand the sequence in which the components unfold most naturally. Consider how a tennis coach teaches new players to hit the ball using a logical sequence: step forward, move the racket back, make contact with the ball, follow through. Once players get these basics automatically, they hit forehand and backhand shots in one fluid motion. That makes tennis (and deep ministry for that matter) more organic and even messier at times—but a whole lot more fun and effective.

So as we break down each step in the Deep Design process—while dropping into the template a practical example that will allow you to see Deep Design "in action"—consider this chapter your primer on your way to doing deep ministry much more fluidly, organically, and naturally.

DEEP DESIGN, STEP 1 (DISCERNMENT): *NOW?*

We youth workers often function like emergency rescue workers—responding to the latest 911 call from a kid after dousing the remaining fires that sprang up at last night's youth group meeting. We often get so busy *doing* ministry that we lose sight of what God is doing now *in* our ministries.

Step 1 invites us to slow down and discern what God is up to in our ministries **Now**. This begs an obvious question: *what exactly is "God's activity"?* Academics and theologians sometimes use the word *telos* to describe God's actions. In this context the Greek word *telos* means God's divine intentions or purposes.

That helps somewhat, but we're still left with the question of what God intends: is it the advancement of his kingdom? The reign of his peace? That all people worship him? Yes, to all of these—but in its simplest essence, God

What's that cross doing in the middle of the Deep Design?

In the midst of our Deep Design, we want our reflection and the intersection between our ministries and others' insights to be continually filtered through the lens of God's activity. How do we know if we're aligning ourselves with God's activity? While our finite brains prevent us from ever fully knowing, one way we understand God's activity is through his revelation, which we know primarily from Scripture. We've placed the cross at the heart of our Deep Design as a reminder that we want all of our personal and ministry reflection to revolve around the model and grace of Christ as a central example of God's activity.[2]

---

[2]Had we been gearing this as an academic text, we would have labeled this filter "Christopraxis," meaning that our "praxis," or theologically grounded practice, is determined by God's activity as seen through Christ.

intends **transformation**. He desires this transformation to happen on multiple levels—in our individual lives, in our churches and communities, and in our larger world. (We'll dive more deeply into the relationship between our individual and communal transformation in Chapter 4.)

One scriptural passage that helps us understand more about the transformation God intends is Romans 12:1-2. After urging his readers in Rome to be "living sacrifices, holy and pleasing to God" in verse 1, the two commands in verse 2 shed interesting light on the transformation process. Paul uses the imperative verb phrase "Do not conform any longer to the pattern of this world…"—in a sense telling the reader, "Stop allowing yourself to be conformed." And yet, in his next command to "be transformed," the verb is in the passive voice, clearly suggesting that God is the one who does the transformation in us. So while we agree that God's grace, love, and power are core to transformation, we as humans still have some participative role—albeit small—in it.

In our Deep Design, the goal of the first step is to discern God's transformation in our midst today. More specifically, we ask three **Now** subquestions:

1. What type of transformation is God bringing about now?

2. What is creating space for God's transformation now?

3. What is hindering God's transformation now?

We spent a lot of time with the wording for questions 2 and 3. We wanted to avoid phrases that made it seem as though God is completely dependent upon us, yet at the same time we wanted to avoid terms that made it seem we have no role whatsoever. "Creating space" and "hindering" are the best we've come up with—but please feel free, as you apply these questions to your own ministry, to come up with terms that better capture your own theology.

STEP 1: NOW?

GOAL: To discern God's current transformation by asking:

- What type of transformation is God bringing about now?
- What is creating space for God's transformation now?
- What is hindering God's transformation now?

So what's the process for answering these three **Now** sub-questions? The short answer is through experience. But not just *your* experience as a youth leader. We're talking about *collective experience.* It's impossible for any individual to alone see the true reality of anything, let alone the complicated whirlpool we call youth ministry. We need the insights of others in our community as we reflect on our shared experience. So hopefully you can invite other adult leaders, parents, and students to be part of your **Now** conversation.

In your personal reflections and communal discussions, it's helpful to consider your ministry from the perspective of God's story as presented in Scripture: *where in your ministry do you see actions and attitudes that resemble Jesus' life and ministry? Where in your community are the passions of Jesus being expressed?* Poignant answers to these questions are often revealed through corporate prayer, spiritual disciplines, worship, and discussions about God's narrative presented in Scripture.

If possible, we recommend that you include the perspectives of those outside your ministry setting to give you an even broader collective experience. By reading others' writings, attending ministry gatherings, or dialoguing with colleagues in other ministries, you can gain a broader sense of God's transforming activity in your midst and how you are and are not participating.

DEEP DESIGN, STEP 1 IN ACTION: OUR SMALL GROUPS NOW

(For the purposes of demonstrating the Deep Design in action, we'll consider hypothetically how Kara's church might examine the small group portion of its youth program.)

After spending time in personal reflection and discussion, I might be able to offer the following responses to the **Now** questions regarding our small groups:

What type of transformation is God bringing about now?

After months of our prayerful recruiting, God has provided enough small group leaders. God seems to be bringing a few new students to our ministry every month who want to be connected in small groups.

What is creating space for God's transformation now?

We offer small group leaders some initial training in September that is very thorough and practical; some of our small group leaders are integrating brief times of worship (with and without music) into their meetings that students are enjoying.

DEEP MINISTRY

What is hindering God's transformation now?

Many of our new leaders are young and are asking for more mentoring and coaching than we're currently providing; small group leaders and members often tell us the relationships in their groups are pretty shallow; students don't seem all that interested in studying Scripture, and small group leaders are getting frustrated with their kids' apathy; small groups are pretty focused on themselves and aren't serving those on the outside.

The great theologian Woody Allen once said, "80 percent of success is showing up." This first step of figuring out the **Now** of your ministry helps you evaluate who (and what!) is showing up in the first place.

DEEP DESIGN, STEP 2 (REFLECTION): *NEW?*

The goal of Step 2 is to reflect upon **New** ideas and insights that speak to the issues that arose as you discerned God's activity in your ministry **Now** (Step 1).

How can we identify the **New** ideas that can help move our ministries out of the shallow end? We can gain wisdom from those both inside and outside our contexts by asking four subquestions:

- What does Scripture say?

- What does history say?

- What does research say?

- What does experience say?[3]

---

[3] There are obvious parallels between these four subquestions and the well-known Wesleyan Quadrilateral. Based largely on the writings of John Wesley, the Wesleyan Quadrilateral teaches that God's revelation comes in four forms: Scripture, tradition, reason, and experience. Two of our **New** subquestions match the Wesleyan Quadrilateral in their focus on Scripture and experience. We have changed "tradition" to "history" because for many the word *tradition* means only current traditions while *history* more clearly communicates the thinking and practices of the church throughout its existence. We have changed "reason" to "research" to send the message that we want to gain **New** insights from others' research and not just from our individual rationality.

STEP 1: NOW?

GOAL: To discern God's current transformation by asking:

- What type of transformation is God bringing about now?
- What is creating space for God's transformation now?
- What is hindering God's transformation now?

STEP 2: NEW?

GOAL: To reflect upon new insights and ideas by asking:

- What does Scripture say?
- What does history say?
- What does research say?
- What does experience say?

What Does Scripture Say?

Scripture has two types of authority. One is its historical authority—it contains God's commands to people in biblical times. The second is its normative authority, meaning that when properly interpreted, the Bible helps us understand God's commands to us today. This also means that if Scripture says one thing, and something or someone else says another, we believe Scripture trumps that other voice.

But since Scripture has been around for so long, is there anything **New** we can find in it? Well, yes and no. Scripture is timeless, so it doesn't change. But by examining Bible commentaries and other great thinkers who've tried to understand specific texts, we gain a larger and clearer sense of God's truth. We often skim Scripture and draw merely a surface-level sense of its meaning and power. But if we treat it like a great poem, if we meditate further upon its beauty and significance, we'll keep learning **New** insights—not just about the scene being described, but the One doing the writing.

What Does History Say?

By "history," we mean traditions and teachings from the past. In our hunt for "fresh" ideas, we in youth ministry often disregard the "outdated" wisdom of those who've studied and served God before us, as if nothing significant has happened since the Bible was written thousands of years ago. Whether because of our ignorance or pride, we've turned a collective deaf ear to the whispers of wisdom from the past. Studying our history helps clear the wax from our ears.

Whether your church and youth ministry have been around for 100 years or one month, they are undoubtedly grounded in certain beliefs and traditions. Perhaps you need to abandon these historical principles and practices. Maybe even more likely you need to hold firm to them and re-**New** them by translating them in fresh ways that make sense to your students. Either way, we can truly bring change only as we value the church and work within the narrative of the church's own self-understanding.

What Does Research Say?

We move from the past to the present through the third voice in finding **New** depth: research. When we talk

In trying to hear from Scripture, history, research, and experience, there are times when one or two voices will have more to contribute to your Deep Design than others. Sometimes Scripture shouts about an issue; other times it whispers. Occasionally history has volumes of insight; often it is silent. That's okay. It's unrealistic to expect each source to contribute exactly 25 percent to your process. Nothing that matters in life is that neat and clean. As we'll see in the chapters that follow, the goal is to soak in wisdom from all four when possible, not to artificially squeeze a few drops from a source that's actually pretty dry on a particular issue.

about "research," we're generally referring to studies in social-science fields such as communication, psychology, education, anthropology, and sociology.

Now, we know that many of you believe that research is done by boring scientists in white lab coats who study irrelevant questions and end up giving purple pills to one half of the guinea pigs and green pills to the rest. But that's not the kind of research we're talking about. We're talking about Roll-Up-Your-Sleeves-with-Kids research. We're talking about research that puts adults in the position of listeners and students in the position of youth-culture experts. We're talking about what is now being referred to in academic circles as "action research," meaning research that reflects the real needs of real people and offers real help. Overlooking these contributions in your search for deeper ministry is a little bit like looking for a dime in the dark. You might find it, but it sure takes a lot longer.

What Does Experience Say?

We move from others' insights back to your own through the fourth voice in finding **New** depth: experience. Your church, your community, and your kids are unlike any others. You as a leader are unlike any other leader. God intends to use all of these unique experiences to help you swim past shallow waters. By putting your experiences under a microscope, you'll see the tiny nuances and hidden principles that you might otherwise miss.

DEEP DESIGN, STEP 2 IN ACTION: *NEW* INSIGHTS ABOUT OUR SMALL GROUPS

In defining our **Now** (the first Deep Design step), I realized that while our youth program has enough small group leaders, the groups are not reaching their full po-

tential. The teaching in our small groups is stagnant, and the relationships in them are superficial. Our small group leaders also want more mentoring and training than we're currently providing. With all those evaluations in the back of my mind, now I'm going to seek out some relevant **New** insights about community and small groups.

What does Scripture say? While the Bible never mentions "small groups," it says plenty about the types of intimate relationships God wants. Let's look at a description of life in the first century church in Acts 2:42-47: "They devoted themselves to the apostles' teaching" (are we poring over the teachings of Christ like they did?) "and to the fellowship" (are we "devoted" to one another deeply and committed to meeting together regularly?) "and to prayer." (How much time are we spending in corporate prayer?) "Selling their possessions and goods, they gave to anyone as he had need" (are we making sacrifices to meet others' needs?).

Considering these questions raised by Scripture can offer us **New** insights that can bring greater depth to our ministry.

What does history say? One of the great historical lessons about small groups comes from the example and ministry of John Wesley. The heart of Methodism during Wesley's life was covenant groups—a.k.a., "band groups"—of five to 10 people each. Their purpose was to "band" together for intimate, soul-searching examination.[4] On December 25, 1738, Wesley drafted the following questions to be asked at every band group meeting:

1. What known sins have you committed since our last meeting?

2. What temptations have you met?

[4] Michael Henderson, *John Wesley's Class Meeting* (Nappanee, IN: Evangel Publishing House, 1997), 112.

3. How were you delivered?

4. What have you thought, said, or done, of which you doubt whether it be sin or not?

The intentionality and accountability behind these questions are a vital historical example that can deepen our small group ministry today.

What does research say? In an effort to capture their students' interest and attention, McMaster University Medical School, Harvard Medical School, and other academic programs around the country have developed a new approach called "problem-based learning."

As you might guess, in this approach a problem drives the learning. Ideally the problem is one students cannot solve until they gain new skills and/or knowledge. In addition, the problem is immediately relevant to real-life situations they may face. The professors provide the learning environments that support their students' thinking, but it is the learners who take ownership of the process used to arrive at the solution.

The implications for our small group ministry are obvious. As noted in my **Now** discernment, my students don't seem all that interested in studying Scripture. And more often than not, leaders jump into teaching Scripture *assuming students will be motivated just because it's "the Bible."* But a study on the Sermon on the Mount becomes more interesting when connected to the tension of passing a homeless person as you head to church. Examining Shadrach, Meshach, and Abednego is more intriguing in light of the struggle your students might face when friends suggest watching some porn on cable TV.

While problem-based learning helps students remain engaged with their studies, one nagging question about this relatively **New** method is whether students receive enough

  **DEEP MINISTRY**

training in the basic elements of the curriculum. Medical school students in problem-based learning programs occasionally score lower than their more conventionally trained counterparts.[5] Since the problems emerge from students' contexts, perhaps those gaps are due to students' limited experiences. Translating that to youth ministry, your students might end up understanding how the story of Daniel relates to peer pressure but have only a cursory understanding of issues more removed from their daily lives such as poverty, the environment, and the end times.

Given these documented experiences of medical school students as well as our desire to avoid application-driven prooftexting, we in youth ministry probably need a combination of problem-based learning and more traditional Bible study to maximize the effectiveness of our small groups.

What does experience say? Answering this question helps us sort through our own experiences in community to figure out how to develop deeper relationships. Even though it's been more than 20 years since I was in high school, the leader of our small group during that time left a deep mark on me that the years have not erased. First, Kristi asked us to hold her accountable for changes in her life. She asked us to check in with her to see how she was doing at memorizing Scripture and eating more healthily. We had a reciprocal relationship. We needed her, but she needed us, too.

Second, she spent time with us outside our small group meetings. When her husband was out of town, she'd invite us over to spend the night. She'd meet us for dinner, invite us to go shopping, or simply have us over after school to make cookies. The more time we spent with her outside our official small group meeting, the deeper our conversations during our small group time.

---

[5] M.A. Albanese, "Problem-Based Learning: A Review of Literature on its Outcomes and Implementation Issues," *Academic Medicine*, 68, no.8 (August 1993): 615.

DEEP DESIGN, STEP 3 (OBSERVATION): *WHO?*

The goal of Step 3 is to observe others **Who** have come up with **New** insights similar to ours (Step 2) and are already trying to go deeper. These people's willingness to try new ideas and paddle, sidestroke, and freestyle forward can help you take a few bold—or maybe tentative—strokes into deeper waters.

In order to effectively take the third step of the Deep Design process and figure out Who you can learn from—and how their stories relate to your own—you will want to ask three questions:

- What are some ways others are applying these new insights to their ministries?

- In what ways are their situations similar to ours?

- In what ways are they different?

STEP 1: NOW?

GOAL: To discern God's current transformation by asking:

- What type of transformation is God bringing about now?
- What is creating space for God's transformation now?
- What is hindering God's transformation now?

STEP 3: WHO?

GOAL: To observe others who are already going deeper by asking:

- What are some ways others are applying these new insights to their ministries?
- In what ways are their situations similar to ours?
- In what ways are they different?

STEP 2: NEW?

GOAL: To reflect upon new insights and ideas by asking:

- What does Scripture say?
- What does history say?
- What does research say?
- What does experience say?

STEP 3 IN ACTION: *WHO* IS GOING DEEPER IN SMALL GROUPS?

Let's imagine I've been talking with my friend, Blanca, who is already applying some of the **New** insights we learned from Scripture, history, research, and experience.

How is Blanca's youth ministry trying to apply these new insights to her ministry?

She asks each group to do some creative prayer element every time it meets; every three months her small groups do a service project in their community. (Without even knowing it, Blanca's been teaching her small group leaders a "problem-based learning" method.)

In what ways is Blanca's situation similar to ours?

Like our ministry, her group is also growing with new students who want to be connected in small groups; the adult Sunday school classes at her church are very strong, just like at our church.

In what ways is Blanca's situation different?

She intentionally keeps her groups pretty small so it's easier to add new students to them as they join the ministry; our groups are so big that new students feel lost when they show up. She encourages her leaders to do one or two activities every month with their groups outside their normal small group meetings. Blanca has an excellent training manual already developed; we have no training program for our small group leaders after our initial training in September.

By observing the successes and struggles of Blanca (and others) who are incorporating new insights into their programs, and considering the similarities and differences between our situations, we can discover what might work best in our own ministries.

DEEP DESIGN, STEP 4 (APPLICATION): HOW?

Now that we've reflected on **New** depth (Step 2 of our Deep Design diagram) and studied the example of another ministry **Who** is already applying our insights (Step 3), we are well equipped to answer the final synthesizing question: given everything, **How** can we go deeper?

STEP 1: NOW?
GOAL: To discern God's current transformation by asking:

- What type of transformation is God bringing about now?
- What is creating space for God's transformation now?
- What is hindering God's transformation now?

STEP 3: WHO?
GOAL: To observe others who are already going deeper by asking:

- What are some ways others are applying these new insights to their ministries?
- In what ways are their situations similar to ours?
- In what ways are they different?

STEP 4: HOW?
GOAL: To apply information from Steps 1-3 by asking:

- Given everything, how can we go deeper?

STEP 2: NEW?
GOAL: To reflect upon new insights and ideas by asking:

- What does Scripture say?
- What does history say?
- What does research say?
- What does experience say?

While this final step only has one question, it is just as complex as the three previous steps (if not more!) since it integrates and applies all your previous reflection. As you see in the table below, our answer to this one question addresses the issues raised in Step 1 by using the insights that emerged in Steps 2 and 3.

DEEP DESIGN, STEP 4 IN ACTION: *HOW* TO GO DEEPER IN OUR SMALL GROUPS

How we can go deeper in our small groups?	Source
We should ask small groups to do either a creative service project or a creative prayer time every month during their normal meeting times. We'll give them some ideas, or they can come up with their own.	Scripture, Blanca's ministry
We should consider encouraging each small group to develop a few questions about their relationships with God and with others that can be discussed every time they meet.	Scripture, History
We should encourage leaders to come up with potential "problem-based learning" ideas to start their meetings.	Research
We should invite my friend Blanca to come and do some training with our leaders. After all, given the great training procedures she's already developed, why reinvent the wheel?	Research, Blanca's ministry
We can give our leaders some ideas on how to spend time with their groups outside their normal small group meetings.	Experience, Blanca's ministry
We need to consider recruiting more leaders so we can make our groups smaller, allowing new students to join without feeling so intimidated and excluded.	Blanca's ministry
We should choose a few adult Sunday school classes (especially those comprised of parents involved in our youth ministry) and ask them if they would be willing to mentor some of our students.	Blanca's ministry

So what have we just done? We've used insights from Scripture, history, research, and experience, as well as the observations of others' ministries to come up with a custom plan for our ministry. Instead of following any single guide or plan mindlessly, we've figured out where and how to blaze our own trail.

The Goal of This Book: It's Up to *You* to Think It Through!

Our ultimate goal is to help you learn to do deep ministry in a shallow world. Wouldn't that be great? No matter what challenges you face—from apathetic kids to a lack of adult leaders—you can formulate and customize a strategy that gets you out of the kiddie pool and into deeper waters.

Throughout the rest of the book, each chapter follows the same four methodological steps of **Now, New, Who,** and **How.** But the different chapters will do so in different ways. That's because we didn't want to rigidly superimpose our Deep Design method onto the data. We tried to find the best blend between our method and the state of youth ministry and research today. Often the data lends itself to following the four steps in order. Sometimes we've combined a few steps because this seems like the most logical reflection of what youth workers, theologians, and researchers were learning and contributing. After all, it shouldn't be the method that's sitting in the driver's seat—that's God's place. And then it's you, your kids, Scripture, and the wisdom of others that should be closest to the steering wheel.

To make sure you track with the four steps, we've divided each of the remaining chapters into steps—**Now**? **New**? **Who**? and **How**? For the first three steps, we've also placed diagrams and Deep Design Prompts in the margins that help you follow our progress through the Deep Design.

The fourth step is where we invite you to apply the material to your own life and ministry. At the end of every chapter, we've included a few reflection questions and an application table to use with your own ministry and leadership teams.

You might think of each chapter as a jigsaw puzzle. Studying **Now**, **New**, and **Who** is a bit like dumping a box of puzzle pieces on your dining-room table. In the final section, by mulling over some strategic reflection questions, you get to figure out **How** to put those pieces together into a puzzle that fits your ministry. Sure, we'll give you some strong hints—but we believe God will show you and your team the best "picture" for your students. Our hope is that by the end of this book, following the Deep Design will be as intuitive as breathing—you'll do it without realizing it.

Odds are good you'll get a few ideas from each chapter. You might decide to focus primarily on a few chapters that best address the needs of your own kids and families. In fact, that might be a really smart move—trying to make too many changes at once is tiring for you and everyone else connected to your ministry.

A Few Final Tidbits for You "Process"-Oriented Youth Workers

If you're one of those "bottom line" youth workers who likes things short, sweet, and straightforward, then you may want to skip right to the application questions at the end of this chapter. We've already given you a full explanation of the Deep Design.

But if you're one of those "process"-oriented youth workers who not only loves getting your hands dirty but also wants to know what kind of dirt your hands are in—and how other people feel about that dirt—then this section is for you. We want to give you a backstage pass to the process that has gone into the development

of Deep Design and explain some of the choices we made in this book.

What role does experience play in the Deep Design? In Step 1, we encourage you to use collective experience as the means to engage with and answer the three **Now** questions. In Step 2, we urge you to reflect upon your experience in order to gain **New** insight. While experience has an explicit role in both of those steps, let's be honest that the role of experience doesn't end there. How we read Scripture, understand history, integrate research, observe and compare others' ministries with our own, and apply those insights to our own settings are all colored by our experiences. That's okay. In fact, it's good when we acknowledge the impact of our experiences and assess whether they are helpful or harmful.

Why are we trying to integrate so many academic disciplines? If you read these chapters carefully, you'll pick up threads of Systematic Theology, Historical Theology, Practical Theology, Psychology, Education, Communication, Sociology, Missiology, and a few other "ologies" to boot. That's because no single discipline has the corner on the market of ministering to your kids. We decided to mine the wealth offered by a variety of disciplines so you could approach your kids and your ministry in the most holistic way possible.

At times that means we can't delve as deeply into any one of those disciplines as we'd like—or maybe as deeply as you would like. But we felt the benefit of integrating research, theories, and practices from a variety of fields was worth the potential sacrifice.

But don't various academic disciplines approach studying people differently, and don't they sometimes contradict one another? Well, yes and yes. After all, they often operate on different assumptions and thus develop different methodologies. But they don't contradict one another as much as you might think when addressing the topics covered in this book. When differing fields do seem to offer conflicting evidence (such as in Chapter 6 on mentoring), we've tried to suggest explanations that resolve some of the differences without diluting the impact of their respective findings.

Why do we occasionally blend the content of Steps 3 and 4? As you read the rest of this book, you'll probably notice that, at times, some of the questions for Step 3 appear in Step 4. The reality is that there is significant overlap between others **Who** are applying the **New** information, and **How** you will apply it. As you become adept at applying the Deep Design to your ministry, you can choose for yourself where to turn the corner to application—and how sharply or gradually you want to take that turn.

Why do we order the steps as we do? Some colleagues suggested that we put the **Who** step before the **New** step. While it's true that you will partially consider other ministries as you discern God's transforming activity, we were concerned that placing the entire **Who** step so early in the Deep Design would short-circuit the process. If readers had already gained a few quick answers from other leaders, they might be tempted to skip over the valuable work of sifting through what Scripture, history, research, and experience have to say.

It's also been suggested that we skip or abbreviate the **Now** step so readers could spend more time in the **New** and **Who** sections. Yet we felt it was important to encourage youth workers to begin with a thorough examination of the present ministry practices and impact, since so few youth workers take time with their teams to discern what God is doing in their ministries.

Are the steps really as linear as you suggest? As you're starting the Deep Design, we encourage you to follow the steps in the order we've outlined. But once you become a Deep Design expert, you'll probably find yourself moving through the various steps intuitively. Sometimes you might even want to ping-pong back and forth between **Now** and **New** to help you go deeper and deeper in your practices and reflection. In practical theology circles, that type of back and forth between practice and reflection is called a "praxis-theory-praxis" feedback loop.

What's the difference between "practice" and "praxis"? It's more than just a few letters of the alphabet. In practical theology, what separates "praxis" from "practice" is that "praxis" includes some sort of purpose, or "telos," behind the activity.

If it makes sense for you to reorder the steps to suit better how you think and act, by all means, go for it. Be creative and have fun. Just please don't skip too much.

The exciting news is that there is an ocean of new depth ahead.

And you get to help navigate it!

Application Questions:

1. Who from your ministry should you involve in these Deep Design discussions?

2. We recommend that you try answering the three questions in Step 1 for your ministry overall before you move to the next chapter. So...what type

of transformation is God bringing about? What is creating space for this transformation? What is hindering it?

3. We also recommend that you develop a sense of your unique community and ministry before you read any further. So…what are your students like? How about their parents? How would you describe the adult leaders in your ministry? What about your church? How would you describe the community in which you live and serve?

4. Look again at the table of contents for this book. Given your answers to questions 2 and 3, which chapters in this book do you expect will be especially relevant to you?

5. What role does Scripture usually play in finding **New** ideas for your ministry? What role do you want it to play? If there is a difference in your answers, what does this tell you?

6. Do you agree that history, research, and experience are all important ways to learn **New** insights? Why or why not?

7. **Who** in ministry have you tended to follow in the past? When, if at all, did you diverge from their models, and why did you decide to branch out on your own journey?

CHAPTER 3

DEEP CHANGE: WHERE MIGHT I GO WRONG, AND WHERE CAN I GO RIGHT?

Kara Powell

DEEP DESIGN, STEP 1 (DISCERNMENT): *NOW?*

Suppose someone you respect observed your ministry, then gave you this warning—"Your ministry is shallow. If it doesn't change, it will die." At that point, you'd change, right? Actually, you probably wouldn't. You'd likely fall in with the majority of people who fail to make changes even when the stakes are as high as you can imagine.

Every day people fail to make changes **Now**, even when their own lives are on the line. According to Dr. Edward Miller, dean of the medical school and CEO of the hospital at Johns Hopkins University, about 600,000 people in the United States have heart bypasses every year, and 1.3 million heart patients have angioplasties, all at a total cost of around $30 billion. These procedures relieve chest pains temporarily but are not viewed as long-term solutions. About half the time bypass grafts clog up within a few years and angioplasties often need redoing after a few months.

Many patients could avoid repeating the surgery, as well as address their actual heart disease, by adopting healthier lifestyles. Yet very few do. Miller summarizes, "If you look at people after coronary-artery bypass grafting two years later, 90% of them have not changed their lifestyles."[6]

It's not because these patients don't know the basic steps to better health. In all likelihood their friends and doctors have warned them to start exercising and cut back on smoking, drinking, stress, and unhealthy eating. I'd even be willing to guess that many (perhaps most) of them have tried to obey their doctors' orders. But the path to healthy eating is laden with burgers and fries, and the path to exercise is blocked by the all-too-comfortable couch.

[6]Alan Deutschman, "Change or Die," *Fast Company* 94 (May 2005) :53.

Change or die. Tragically, most people end up sabotaging their progress now because they don't have what it takes to make changes that would save their lives later. So let's be honest: change is hard. All growth requires some kind of pain. Even when it's only your own behavior that needs changing, you still might not be able to do it.

 **DEEP DESIGN PROMPT**

Hindering God's transformation: Change is hard work—even if it's just changing *ourselves.*

But we're asking you to do something even harder. As you walk through the Deep Design process in each chapter, you'll likely realize that students, parents, adult staff, and your entire church community need to change as much as you. Maybe even more. So you're not up against only your own resistance to change—you're up against theirs, too.

Deep Change: A Tale of Two Chances

I've learned the hard way how tough it is to bring about deep change. A few years ago we decided we needed to clarify the vision of our junior high ministry. So the four paid staff members read a book about youth ministry vision and then met for two hours to talk about it. We agreed that we liked the book's ideas, but some of the words didn't fit our students. After spending about 15 minutes brainstorming better words, we congratulated ourselves for coming up with "our" new vision statement so quickly.

At the next staff meeting, we presented our new vision statement to our adult volunteers. We shared it with our students the following Sunday. At our next parents meeting, we told them about it. We invited everyone to memorize it so they could better partner with us.

I don't think a single one of them memorized it.

Truth be told, neither did I.

For one thing, it was too long. Plus, we had come up with it so quickly that I didn't really feel like I owned it.

We lost sight of that vision statement. (Big surprise, eh?) Every four or five months, an adult volunteer would ask, "Whatever happened to that vision statement you guys gave us?" I'd usually shrug and say, "It's still around here somewhere." We tried to change our ministry by coming up with a creative and provocative vision statement, but we ended up with words on a page that got buried somewhere in my file cabinet.

∞ DEEP DESIGN PROMPT

Creating space for God's transformation: Giving us second (and third, and fourth!) chances to make changes effectively.

Six months ago God provided me with a second chance. The high school pastor at our church invited my husband and me to help the youth ministry create a new vision statement. This time I was determined to follow the Deep Design process.

To answer the three **Now** questions about God's transformation and how we were facilitating or hindering it, we held a series of focus groups with students, parents, adult volunteers, and graduates (see Chapter 12 for more on how you can do the same in your ministry). My husband and I wrote up the results and shared them with the high school pastor and the entire volunteer team at the next staff retreat.

Since there were 40 adults on the high school volunteer team, we agreed that we needed a specific Vision Team of 10 adults to explore **New** sources of depth. To glean all we could from Scripture, history, research, and experience, my husband and I asked the Vision Team to read chapters from a handful of books on vision and mission and then come together to discuss what we'd learned. We also discussed other leaders **Who** had developed similar visions, seeking to find what we could learn from them and how we needed to modify their examples.

To test whether we were on the right track, we presented our initial ideas to our student leadership team and the remaining 30 adult leaders. They gave us the green light

to keep going, so the Vision Team met again to determine **How** to actually phrase and implement our new vision. We spent a few hours brainstorming not only the final content but also visual images that would help our students really embrace our direction. Finally, we talked about **How** to explain the vision to the overall church, to students and their families, and to adult leaders who hadn't been such an integral part of the process.

This second time we got it right. We involved the right people, we took the right amount of time, and we followed the right steps.

Odds are good that your ministry will not literally "die" tomorrow if you don't make major changes immediately. But maybe it's getting sick, or perhaps it's in need of a thorough physical. The longer you wait to address its health, the more likely your students are to drift away without experiencing the Divine Healer. Whether your ministry needs a minor check-up or major surgery, there is a deeper and more abundant life waiting for you and your students when you open yourself to the process of change.

DEEP DESIGN, STEP 2 (REFLECTION): *NEW?*

It's time for a group confession: we youth workers aren't known for our savvy when it comes to leading ministry changes. Some of us act like Lone Rangers and try to bring about change ourselves. Others walk into important meetings with people who might resist change (including the pastors and committees who supervise us!) as if we were preparing for a final showdown at the O.K. Corral.

What's wrong with those approaches? They represent lousy change processes. Even if we have the best idea ever, if we can't communicate it with others so they get on board with us, we may as well be sending out smoke signals.

∞ DEEP DESIGN PROMPT

STEP 1: NOW?   STEP 3: WHO?

STEP 4: HOW?   **STEP 2: NEW?**

∞ DEEP DESIGN PROMPT

Experience: We youth workers aren't known for our savvy in making changes.

DEEP DESIGN PROMPT

Experience: Even the best Deep Design will fail without vital Change Principles.

Our four-step Deep Design is incomplete if a healthy process doesn't surround it. Many attempts at change fail not because the leaders lack ideas, but because of poor communication and process. Here are some vital "Change Principles" to help you avoid the common pitfalls.

Change Principle 1: Get People Involved

If I had to choose one Scripture passage to summarize how to effectively involve people in the changes associated with your Deep Design, it would be Ephesians 4:11-12a. In these verses, Paul writes the church of Ephesus, "It was he [God] who gave some to be apostles, some to be prophets, and some to be evangelists, and some to be pastors and teachers, *so these leaders could do all the works of service themselves.*"

Huh? Wait, that doesn't sound quite right. Let's try it again.

"It was he who gave some to be apostles, some to be prophets, some to be evangelists, and some to be pastors and teachers, *to prepare God's people for works of service.*"

DEEP DESIGN PROMPT

Scripture: I act most like a minister when others do the ministry.

Ah, that sounds more like it. According to Paul, you're doing your best job as a leader when others are involved in service. You are acting most like a pastor when you help others engage fully in ministry.

This first-century teaching was lost as the church grew in power and scope. Instead of the priest being the one who helped others do ministry, the priest became the one who *did* the ministry. As a result a great separation developed between those who had "spiritual" vocations (priests) and those who had "worldly" vocations (everyone else).

This chasm was exemplified in the distinctions between the priest and the people that guided communion

practices in the Middle Ages—the priest was at the altar, the people came to the altar rail; the priest stood, but the people kneeled; the priest took the bread and wine, but the people received only the bread. In summarizing the overall climate of the 16th century, Martin Luther writes, "Whoever looked at a monk fairly drooled in devotion and had to be ashamed of his secular station in life."[7]

DEEP DESIGN PROMPT

History: In the Middle Ages, there was a great divide between the power and prestige of priests and the rest of the faith community.

In an effort to reclaim Paul's teachings about the role of priests in the community, Luther taught that believers do not need a priest or a pope to approach God but can commune with God directly all by themselves. Yet this journey is far from individualistic; each believer's direct communion with God is enhanced and enabled by the community of the church. Thus all members of the community serve as priests for one another, or in Luther's words, "all Christians are priests, and all priests are Christians."[8] By this deep teaching known as the "priesthood of all believers," Luther leveled the ministerial playing field.

This historical teaching helps us invite full input from other members, or priests, in our communities as we seek deep change in our ministries with youth. At the very least they should give input; but your change process will be even more effective if these members are part of the decision process. Those of us who are "take charge" youth workers need to ask hard questions: *Do I view my students and adult leaders as voices through whom the Holy Spirit is speaking? Or do I think of them as people who merely carry out what the Holy Spirit has shown me?*

Do we *really* listen to others in our ministries because we understand that they have valuable perspectives that we need to hear? Or do we only pretend to listen to them as a way to get them on our sides and ensure their support for *our own ideas?*

---

[7]Edward Plass, *What Luther Says* (Nutley, NJ: Craig, 1973), 1:4.
[8]*Luther's Works* Volume 40 (St. Louis: Concordia, 1958), 19.

Trust us, your team members can tell if you truly value them and sincerely want to hear from them or if you're faking it. Rushing ahead with your own ideas without involving others and their input might bring a few short-term wins, but in the end you'll probably lose more ground than you've gained.

Change Principle 2: Figure Out Your Reasons

After interviewing more than 400 people from 130 organizations, John P. Kotter claims that most organizations make one crucial mistake in trying to help their teams make changes: they don't give vivid reasons for the change. They give people data to changes their opinions instead of showing them truth that will influence their feelings. In other words, these leaders speak to the head instead of the heart.

One of Kotter's examples—a visual, provocative explanation of why change is needed—is so powerful that we want to offer it here in the words of Jon Stegner, the manufacturing CEO who shared the story during his interview.

> We had a problem with our whole purchasing process. I was convinced that a great deal of money was being wasted and would continue to be wasted into the future, and that we didn't even know how much money was being thrown away…
>
> To get a sense of the magnitude of the problem, I asked one of our summer students to do a small study of how much we pay for the different kinds of gloves used in our factories and how many different gloves we buy. I chose one item to keep it simple, something all the plants use and something we can all easily relate to.

When the student completed the project, she reported that our factories were purchasing 424 different kinds of gloves. *Four hundred and twenty four.* Every factory had their own supplier and their own negotiated price. The same glove could cost $5 at one factory and $17 at another. Five dollars or even $17 may not seem like much money, but we buy *a lot* of gloves, and this was just one example of our purchasing problem.

The student was able to collect a sample of every one of the 424 gloves. She tagged each one with the price on it and the factory it was used in…We gathered them all up and put them in our boardroom one day. Then we invited all the division presidents to come visit the room. What they saw was a large, expensive table, normally clean or with a few papers, now stacked with gloves. Each of our executives stared at this display for a minute. Then each said something like, "We buy all these different types of gloves?"

The demonstration quickly gained notoriety. The gloves became part of a traveling road show. They went to every division. They went to dozens of plants. Many, many people had the opportunity to look at the stacks of gloves. The road show reinforced at every level of the organization a sense of "this is how bad it is."[9]

Maybe some of the following ideas can help you think about creative ways to illustrate why something must be done in your own ministry:

- Videotape students offering their honest input about how your ministry is doing.

[9] John P. Kotter, *The Heart of Change* (New York: Harvard Business School Press, 2002), 29-30.

- Invite students in your community who don't come to your youth group to attend one of your meetings. Then have your team take them out for pizza afterward so you can hear what they thought was good and what they thought stunk.

- Ask some of your students or adults to visit other ministries and come back and share what they saw, heard, and experienced.

- Invite the team members involved in your change process to imagine that they are parents, students who don't feel connected to your ministry, or students who don't know Jesus yet. Ask them to imagine that they've come to a youth service or event. What would they experience? How would they feel? Have them journal their answers and then share them with the group.

- Give your kids cameras and ask them to take pictures of people or events that represent the needs of kids in your community. Discuss the pictures to see what changes you might need to make in order to better love and serve kids near your church.

Change Principle 3: What Are the Forces at Work?

As you're flowing through the Deep Design process and identifying where you are **Now**, important **New** insights, and models **Who** you can learn from, you need to ask yourself two key questions: *What forces will resist change?* and *What forces will drive change?*

According to Kurt Lewin, these two types of forces stand in opposition to each other and together create a force field.[10]

[10] Kurt Lewin, *Field Theory in Social Science*:1 *Selected Theoretical Papers*, ed. D. Cartwright (New York: Harper and Row, 1951).

DEEP MINISTRY

Diagram 3.1: Forces Involved in Launching Change

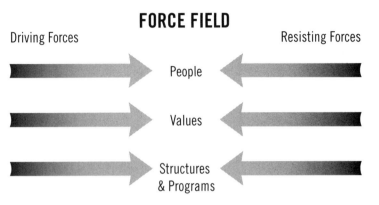

FORCE FIELD

Driving Forces   Resisting Forces

People

Values

Structures & Programs

To modify a famous *Star Wars* quote, you want the right forces to be with you. In other words, you want to increase the driving forces and minimize the resisting forces.

As you'll note in Diagram 3.1, both driving and resisting forces generally fall into three categories:

1. People—particular students, parents, adult staff, church leaders, and members of your community.

2. Values—beliefs and principles that your ministry holds dear.

3. Structures and programs—services, meetings, activities, and ministry programs already in place that could serve either as catalysts for or obstacles to your change.

For a more in-depth look at forces involved in bringing new changes and innovations to your ministry, check out www.cyfm.net.

In Diagram 3.1, the arrows are equal in size, but a longer or shorter arrow would reflect a stronger or weaker force. (If you are more numbers-oriented than arrows-oriented, you could assign each force a numeric value between 1 and 5.)

The "Niners"

A few years ago we considered a major change in our youth ministry. Since many of our eighth graders were getting lost in the shuffle during the transition to high school, we wondered if we should start a separate ministry for freshmen during that first summer and fall called "Niners." The goals of the Niners ministry were to ease the transition for the incoming freshmen and develop the leadership skills of the high school seniors whom we'd ask to lead the Niners ministry. A Force Field diagram for our decision looked something like this:

Diagram 3.2: Forces Involved in Launching Niners

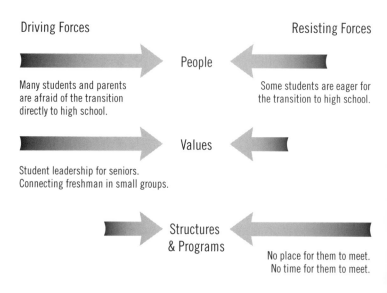

Driving Forces

Resisting Forces

People

Many students and parents are afraid of the transition directly to high school.

Some students are eager for the transition to high school.

Values

Student leadership for seniors.
Connecting freshman in small groups.

Structures & Programs

No place for them to meet.
No time for them to meet.

After studying the forces shaping this new ministry, we knew what we needed to do: figure out how to get on board those who couldn't wait to go to high school and find a place and time to meet. Thanks largely to the momentum provided by the new ministry's resonance with our values, we knew we were on the right track.

Drawing a Force Field diagram accomplishes two goals. First, it shows you the assets that can help with your change (in this case, our values and those nervous freshmen). Second, it shows you the obstacles you need to address as you make your change (in this case, the fact that no adult class wanted a bunch of 14-year-olds meeting next to them on Sunday mornings). As you figure out which forces are like the wind in your sails—and which are like the wind in your face—you'll be able to better navigate the seas of change.

Change Principle 4: Meaningfully Communicate Your Message

Even if your vision for change is perfect, your change may be too shallow if you fail to communicate your message to others in empathetic and meaningful ways.

Often when we sense that others might resist the change we desire, we avoid their tough questions. When we do sit down with them, we often make the mistake of becoming defensive or belittling their concerns and minimizing the risks. But a commitment to sending clear messages enables us to fight against these defeating tendencies and communicate our Deep Design to others.

One of the many reasons we've placed history in our **New** reflection is because of its value in helping others understand the importance of our proposed changes. When we understand both church history in general and the specific history of our own congregation, we're able to discuss why we've done what we've done in the past, and why our ministry needs to be reformed and reshaped. As we explain the changes that are coming, it's important to couch them in a sense of the organic unfolding of events in our community. In many cases, the added depth we're trying to bring to our ministries is more like adding the next ring to the tree trunk instead of uprooting the tree and planting it elsewhere.

In communicating the need for change, it's equally important that we explain what should *not* change. There are undoubtedly elements of your current ministry that God is using to transform students. Taking the time to identify and affirm them can help others in your ministry and church affirm the new directions you need to pursue.

∞ DEEP DESIGN PROMPT

Experience: The more you involve others in spreading your change message, the more likely others will get on board.

You can communicate the message in a variety of forms: through e-mail, handwritten notes, meetings, videos, Power Point® presentations, dramas, role plays, and art. Ideally you won't be the only one doing the communicating—you'll invite other strategic voices to help spread the message. If you're talking to parents, perhaps you should invite one of them to help explain the change. If you're talking to student leaders, another student might better explain the change.

∞ DEEP DESIGN PROMPT

Experience: The time you spend communicating up front will save you time in the end.

But what about all the time it takes to communicate with others? Won't that slow you down? For all you time-conscious youth workers, the good news is that the time you spend in communication in the beginning will actually save you time in the end—and will give you more time overall. The more you explain changes and give people opportunities to ask tough questions in the early stages, the less resistance you'll get later on.

DEEP MINISTRY

DEEP DESIGN, STEP 3 (OBSERVATION): *WHO?*

∞ DEEP DESIGN PROMPT

STEP 1: NOW?   STEP 3: WHO?

STEP 4: HOW?   STEP 2: NEW?

Typically at this point in the Deep Design process, we share stories of youth workers **Who** have applied the **New** ideas to their own ministries. They've moved from armchair quarterbacking to gutting it out on the field of play. In every other chapter in this book, we offer you the chance to think about ways your story is similar to and different from that of other youth workers, and **How** God might want to take your ministry deeper.

But this chapter is a bit different. We felt we couldn't go any further without taking a closer look at the Ultimate Youth Worker. We thought it was time to see what Jesus has to say about change, and how that relates to a deeper ministry.

For being the primo change agent in all of history, Jesus says surprisingly little about change. But in Matthew 18, he gives us a great picture of how to view ourselves in the midst of any change process or Deep Design. While in Capernaum, Jesus' disciples approach him and ask, "Who is the greatest in the kingdom of heaven?" Ever concerned about power and position, the disciples are wondering who will be the top dog.

If I had been Jesus, I'd have been looking for something to throw at them. How could they be wondering about the heavenly hierarchy so shortly after he'd told them he would be betrayed and killed (Matthew 17:22-23)? Are they so insensitive that they care more about their pecking order than Jesus' imminent death?

Instead of getting violent, Jesus gets visual. He calls a little child to them and has the child stand in their midst. Then Jesus warns the disciples, "I tell you the truth, unless you change and become like little children, you will never enter the kingdom of heaven" (Matthew 18:3).

Understanding how children were viewed at the time makes Jesus' admonition to become like them even more startling. In the Greco-Roman world, children were among the least-valued members of society. If I were a disciple who'd just heard Jesus' words, I'd wonder: *What's so great about being a child? How can inferiority be my ticket into the kingdom? How low do I have to go to follow this Jesus?*

Jesus goes on to explain that "whoever humbles themselves like this child is the greatest in the kingdom of heaven" (Matthew 18:4).

Jesus gave his followers a picture of his goal for them: that they would humble themselves. That like children who are dependent on others for their very lives, the disciples would recognize that they, too, are dependent on Jesus for eternal life in the future and earthly life in the present.

As we learn from Scripture, history, research, and experience in this book, let's agree here and now that all great change comes ultimately from God.

All favor comes from God.

All blessing comes from God.

All deep ministry comes from God.

Children know they need their parents. They hover close to them when they're fearful, and they sprint to them when they're ecstatic. In this book, let's have that same attitude about God. Let's admit to ourselves and everyone else we talk to that we need God. We're desperate for him to show us how to get past shallow waters. If we don't feel all that desperate for God, let's confess that to him and ask him to show us how much we need him (a scary prayer, I know).

Only then will we truly experience the depth God has for our ministries and ourselves. Only when we fully rely on God will we reverse the bleak change statistics we read about earlier in this chapter. As we rely on our Abba "Father," I'm betting he'll help us beat the odds.

DEEP DESIGN, STEP 4 (APPLICATION): HOW?

∞ DEEP DESIGN PROMPT

STEP 1: NOW?   STEP 3: WHO?

STEP 4: HOW?   STEP 2: NEW?

Application Questions:

1. What changes has God brought about in you in this last year?

2. What changes has he brought about in your ministry?

3. Which of the four Change Principles (the People, the Reasons, the Forces, and the Message) is most important for you these days? Why? How could you make some progress in that area in the next month?

4. Think of little children you know well. What would have to change in your life if you would be more like them?

5. What difference would these changes make in the way you lead?

6. How would you like to go deeper in bringing about change?

How are we going to go deeper in bringing about change?	Source

CHAPTER 4

DEEP DISCIPLESHIP: WHY ISN'T "DISCIPLESHIP" WORKING LIKE IT USED TO?

Chap Clark

∞ DEEP DESIGN PROMPT

STEP 1: NOW?   STEP 3: WHO?

STEP 4: HOW?   STEP 2: NEW?

∞ DEEP DESIGN PROMPT

Creating space for God's transformation: Adults standing alongside kids in the name of Jesus.

DEEP DESIGN, STEP 1 (DISCERNMENT): *NOW?*

In one of his last articles, Mike Yaconelli wrote, "Youth ministry as an experiment has failed."[11] Although the article caused a stir, Mike later told me, "All I want to do is recapture what we used to live and breathe—we hold kids' hands, we listen to their stories, we take them seriously, and somewhere along the way, we bring them to Jesus. That's it. That's youth ministry." His article, he said, was really a plea to get back to our original calling.

> "All I want to do is recapture what we used to live and breathe—we hold kids' hands, we listen to their stories, we take them seriously, and somewhere along the way, we bring them to Jesus. That's it. That's youth ministry."
>
> —MIKE YACONELLI

Today's kids seem tougher to reach, more distant and disconnected. Programs and events don't have the same impact they used to. Spiritual growth seems much slower and more erratic for most young disciples than even a few years ago. Even those kids who are deeply committed to Jesus Christ often seem to have gaping holes in the way they live out their faith compared to adolescent disciples of the past. Whether it's struggles with lifestyle (e.g., substance abuse or sexual behavior) or attitudes they can't seem to or even want to shake (e.g., racism or spiritual arrogance), what we call "discipleship" doesn't seem to be working like it used to.

---

[11] Mike Yaconelli, "The Failure of Youth Ministry," *YouthWorker Journal* (Spring,2003), cited from http://www.youthspecialties.com/articles/Yaconelli/failure.php on August 4, 2005.

What has created such a sweeping shift? No one disputes that our culture has changed dramatically. Whether it's increasing consumerism and self-centeredness or the steady deterioration of the family as a central stabilizing influence, emerging generations are shaped by a vast array of cultural shifts.

But I believe something even more foundational has changed the nature of adolescence itself. Over the last several decades the support, nurture, and guidance adolescents receive (and so desperately need) from adults has eroded. As a result, by the time today's youth reach high school, many have developed a fatalistic cynicism that makes it hard for them to trust adults and adult-run institutions. In addition, for lots of reasons, adolescence is now a much longer journey. The period between childhood and adulthood known as adolescence used to take about five years (from roughly 13 to 18 years of age), but now this transitional time can take as many as 15 years (usually beginning around age 11 and lasting into the mid-20s).[12] Maturity, in every area, simply takes longer to develop today than it once did.[13]

Church and parachurch youth ministries tend to be far more supportive of adolescents and less agenda-driven than nearly every other system in their young lives. But we still represent a huge, often faceless organization—the *church*. Kids perceive us as being more committed to getting them to participate in *our* events and trips than to them as individuals. In my discussions with thousands of students, many have confirmed that this is one reason for their apparent spiritual lethargy and lack of consistent, free, and passionate growth.[14] They simply do not trust the adults who run programs. As much as they may like us, most will hold back at some level because they see us as adults with self-serving agendas.

For more on the lengthening of adolescence, see a free article available at www.cyfm.net.

∞ **DEEP DESIGN PROMPT**

Hindering God's transformation: Two factors affecting kids—Adults are less available today, and adolescence takes longer than it used to.

 ∞ **DEEP DESIGN PROMPT**

Hindering God's transformation: Students don't trust adults like they used to.

---

[12] See Chap Clark, "Theological Uses of Adolescent Development," in Kenda Creasy Dean, Chap Clark, and Dave Rahn (Eds.) *Starting Right*, Grand Rapids, MI: Zondervan/Youth Specialties Academic, 2001.

[13] The research and background for this section are detailed in Chap Clark, *Hurt: Inside the World of Today's Teenagers*, Grand Rapids: Baker Academic, 2004.

[14] In the research for *Hurt*, I discussed this issue directly with several hundred students. While speaking to large groups I have invited them to let me know what they think of these observations. The overwhelming response of kids has been, "This is what we feel. This is what we think."

This is the environment we face as we attempt to "make disciples" of students. They are in the midst of a difficult, long process of discovering who they are. They're convinced that few adults truly care about what they feel or need. And they are convinced that our interest in them is not about them but about us.

So if that is what is happening **Now**, what does it *mean* and *look like* to lead students into deeper faith in today's fragmented and superficial world?

∞ **DEEP DESIGN PROMPT**

STEP 1: NOW?   STEP 3: WHO?

STEP 4: HOW?   **STEP 2: NEW?**

∞ **DEEP DESIGN PROMPT**

Experience: To hit our target, we need a clear view of what we're trying to accomplish.

∞ **DEEP DESIGN PROMPT**

Research: "Theological reflection" helps us stay focused on what God has revealed to us and apply it to our context.

DEEP DESIGN, STEP 2 (REFLECTION): *NEW?*

When we have a clear view of what we are trying to accomplish, we increase our odds of hitting the target in our work with students. Although this may sound ridiculously obvious, in our fast-paced, add-water-and-stir ministry climate, it may not be as clear as we first assume. To have a "deep ministry" goal, we need to get as close as possible to what *God would say* is the goal of youth ministry. (I can hear the groans of dissent across the pages even now—*"Everybody knows what God wants...he wants disciples!"* Okay, okay, we hear you; but hang in there. We want to unpack what it *means* to "make disciples," and how we are called to organize and focus our ministries on that clear mandate.)

The *New* Goal: Making Disciples Who Are at Home in God's Household

Even in the midst of a wildly changing culture, God isn't worried about kids' response to culture or lengthened adolescence. He remains the Good Shepherd, bringing home those he loves. Our task, then, is to do everything in our power to walk in step with Christ and be faithful to his calling as we join in that task. This is called *theological reflection*—making sure that what we say, do, and believe

is consistent with what God has revealed to us. Let's take a deeper look at what Jesus says:

> All authority in heaven and on earth has been given to me. Therefore go and make disciples of all nations, baptizing them in the name of the Father and of the Son and of the Holy Spirit, and teaching them to obey everything I have commanded you. And surely I am with you always, to the very end of the age. (Matthew 28:18-20)

The Great Commission is the most direct and familiar teaching on the call to ministry. But have we done the deep work to make sure we understand what this means in our particular ministry contexts? In youth ministry, all too often we recite this goal confidently and then grab the latest hot program that promises to somehow make it happen. From there it's easy to reduce Jesus' call to a bumper sticker slogan that sounds great but has little real power to touch souls and transform lives. New and creative programs are great, but they must remain *tools* for a much deeper and complex task—to help students hear God's voice and come home to him.

∞ DEEP DESIGN PROMPT

Experience: New and creative programs may be fine in themselves, but they must be tools for a much deeper and complex task—to help students hear God's voice and come home to him.

WHAT THE GOAL OF YOUTH MINISTRY LOOKS LIKE FROM THE NOW TO THE NEW

With the NOW Goal	With the NEW Goal
• Students learn about faith and life from each other and a few adults	• Students learn about faith and life from a wide variety of people of all ages
• Students have each other to help them carry the burdens of life	• Students have several adults who help them carry life's burdens
• Students use their gifts in serving each other	• Students use their gifts in serving the entire Body of Christ
• Students leave the youth ministry with some great memories and good friends	• Students leave youth ministry and smoothly assimilate into the larger church family
• Students have a good foundation upon which they can build their faith	• Students enter congregational life ready to grow as members of the family of God

4.1

Since Matthew 28:18-20 is the passage commonly used to motivate discipleship ministries, let's dig deeply into that text and find out as much as we can about what it says, both in its original context and for us today. As we unpack this passage, we will look at it through these two lenses:

- *What it means* in terms of its original and objective intent, and

- How we *reflect on it* in light of our own ministry context.

The Great Commission: The Goal of Youth Ministry

Jesus came to them...(verse 18)

What It Means: It begins with a reminder that all we know, think, and do is because Jesus has come to us. God didn't stand aloof and e-mail us dictates, decrees, and principles that we're supposed to memorize and mimic robotically. The power and mystery of the gospel is that God *came to us*. Everything he has said and revealed through creation and his Word is expressed and understood in light of his direct promised presence ("I will never leave you..." Hebrews 13:5). And he has not retreated one step from those he loves.

Why It Matters: This passage emphasizes that God's basic method of communicating his love is by *going*. But that's not all—he also *stays*. Because Jesus has promised to be with us as we minister in his name, we are provided with all the resources, insights, and stamina necessary to break through the walls of fear and isolation kids erect. Jesus is there with and for us—and he is with and for our students as well.

"All authority on heaven and earth has been given to me..." (verse 18)

What It Means: Jesus begins by reminding us of his complete and total authority. When Satan tried to entice Jesus to worship him by offering him authority over the kingdoms of the earth, the irony was that Jesus had already been given "all authority on heaven and earth" (see Matthew 11:27). By reminding his disciples of his authority "on heaven and earth," Jesus makes sure we know for whom we work as we go about our ministry business. We do not build Jesus' kingdom—he builds his kingdom. Ultimately. we do not have the authority over the Great Commission, he does. Youth ministry is God's work, and we are invited to the party.

Why It Matters: Some speak of ministry philosophy and strategy as if God called us to go and make disciples, and then he somehow got busy doing other things. But this brief introduction in Matthew 28:18 shows this is simply not true. God is the one who directs and empowers our ministries, and we are invited and encouraged to follow his lead. Our task is not so much to plan a "wild" ministry to students as it is to listen carefully to God's voice, walk humbly and faithfully with him, and resolve to rely on his presence, input, and power in making sure we stay on his track in making disciples.

∞ DEEP DESIGN PROMPT

Scripture: Because Jesus holds all authority, our ministry is actually *his* ministry.

"Therefore go..." (verse 19)

What It Means: Just as Jesus came to us, we are told to *go*. "As you sent me into the world," Jesus prayed at the Last Supper, "I have sent them into the world" (John 17:18). Note that Jesus lays out the process of disciplemaking by telling us first to go; after we have made that step into the world of those we're supposed to serve, *then* we begin the task of making disciples.

Why It Matters: For far too long we have paid scant attention to the *going* part of the call unless we are sending missionaries into the "mission field." Today theologians and church leaders across traditions are finally recognizing that "missions" is not so much what we send a few people to "do" as who we are *all* called to *be*. We are to be *missional* as we live out the call of God on our lives, and the whole world is our mission field.

In a context where most kids don't have much trust in adults or adult-run systems, this is all the more important. To "make disciples" of adolescents, first we must convince them that we come to them without agendas. Adolescents have created a world beneath the surface of the adult landscape, and as outsiders we are not invited into that world—we just sit on the steps of that world. But we stay and rebuild trust so youth can see God's love for them as they are.

If we would go to them and "sit on the steps" of their world, we must create programmatic structures that begin with "going," and then have this spill over into a welcoming attitude in everything we do. Many youth workers call this "going" *contact work*, meaning that adults enter the world of students on their turf to build trusting relationships. The three "levels" of contact work are: be seen, engage in a conversation, and eventually, do something together. Although this method of youth ministry practice has been around for decades,[15] today, "contact work" has degenerated into hanging out with students to whom we're already close. To rebuild trust, we must commit to regular, ongoing contact work with those we're seeking to disciple.

After established contact work, we must maintain the same principle of "going" when kids attend our programs. Everything we do should have a welcoming attitude and spirit about it. From the music to the speaking and teaching

---

[15] These principles of contact work have been the core of Young Life's ministry since the early 1940s. The *idea* of doing contact work has been floating around church-based youth ministry for decades as well, but few youth workers see it as a requisite beginning point in discipling students.

to the small group times, a "going" youth ministry offers safety and warmth throughout every event and program.

"...and make disciples of all nations" (verse 19)

What It Means: We are about to get a little technical, not to show off (although Kara is really smart), but to let you know how important it is to have a good commentary to keep you aligned with what the Bible actually says. In English these three short verses imply that there are four aspects, or goals, to the Great Commission—we are to go, to make disciples, to baptize, and to teach. But of the four verbs, one is the main command (or "imperative"), and the rest are supporting verbs. As you might have guessed, the central verb of the passage—and Jesus' driving point—is the call "to make disciples." The other three verbs—go, baptize, and teach—are the flesh on the bones of this central point. They describe *how* we are to make disciples.

In going deeper, we have to ask just what it is we are supposed to *make*. The word *disciple* is often thought of as some sort of hyperspiritual word that belongs only to Christians. But on the contrary, it is a rather common Greek word that means "learner" or "student." This means that what Jesus asks of us cannot be put into a neat three- or even seven-year curricular box so our students are "done" by the time they graduate. The concept of "discipleship" (or, as one pastor put it, "followership") is a lifelong process of learning what it means to conform ourselves to the purposes of God and his kingdom. At the very least, a deep youth ministry goal has to recognize that in our relatively brief time with students we are only part of the lifelong process of making disciples of Jesus Christ.

∞ DEEP DESIGN PROMPT

Scripture: Making disciples is a lifelong process.

Why It Matters: As we "make disciples" who are lifelong followers of Jesus Christ, there are two dynamic implications we must keep in mind. First, we are compelled to humbly admit that, although we may play important roles

The goal of youth ministry: To serve the body of Christ by inviting adolescents into the church family.

in the process in young believers' lives, we will not be the primary discipling presence throughout their lives.[16] *At best we are partners for a specific season along with the body of Christ.* Since making disciples is a lifelong process that includes many different people and experiences, it makes sense that we should seek to help students recognize that the local expression of that body, the local church, is the community that God has chosen to do his discipling work. In general, youth ministry does not have a very good track record when it comes to connecting kids to the larger body of Christ. In making disciples, the *trajectory* of our goal must be to represent the church as we assimilate students into the larger local body of Christ by the time they graduate from high school.

"baptizing them in(to) the name of the Father and of the Son and of the Holy Spirit, and teaching them to obey everything I have commanded you" (verses 19-20)

What It Means: Although scholars debate various elements of this verse,[17] this passage affirms more than just the creation of a community of peers (like a youth group) that initiates students through the specific ritual of baptism. The inclusion of Jesus' command to "baptize" and "teach to obey" at the end of his commission assumes being drawn "into the name" of God would include becoming a member of God's human family.[18] Thus, a central aspect of our making disciples of youth is to bring them under the nurturing umbrella of the greater body of Christ. In contrast to how we've operated in youth ministry historically—as if the church doesn't matter (or even exist)—the call to baptize "into the name"[19] of God means that we are to encourage young believers to place their lives under the authority of God and into intimate community with his body, the church. So in making disciples, Jesus tells us we are to work hard

---

[16] Granted, we may be the most important people to a few students during a particular season of their lives. But spiritual growth is a process in which God uses lots of people through a plethora of circumstances and seasons in our lives to shape us.

[17] The use of the singular "in the name," for instance, in reference to the Trinity, when the doctrine of the Trinity was still a long way from being formally articulated by the church, creates some interesting discussion.

[18] Donald A. Hagner, Vol. 33B: *Word Commentary: Matthew 14-28*, Word Biblical Commentary. Dallas: Word, 2002.

[19] "Into" is a better rendering of the Greek word *eis* than the more often used "in."

at bringing them into God's family, where they can learn what God invites them to ("obey") and experience Christ's family on earth, including full participation in corporate worship, community life, and baptism.

Jesus' statement also makes it clear we are to make sure our budding disciples are *taught*. Most churches and programs continue at least to nod to this element of discipleship. But what is often missed is the model of teaching Jesus gave to his disciples—stories, teachable moments, and dialogue not delivered from a lectern or through a microphone but more often along a road or on a hillside. We treat teaching as passing on *information about God* rather than helping students to know and follow Jesus ("obey everything I have commanded you"). Jesus tells us the call to make disciples has two components: making sure students are immersed into the life of faith—with *both* their God and the faith community—and helping them to know Christ's "commands."

Why It Matters: Most of us in youth ministry see the goal of making disciples in terms of getting students to come to our events and meetings, teaching them information about what to believe, and "challenging" them to behave as we think a Christian should behave. But expecting students to show up to follow our agenda can actually push them *away* from the true target of youth ministry. Our current practice of adolescent discipleship rarely focuses on the central goal of going to youth with love and acceptance, and then inviting them into the greater body of Christ where they will be loved, trained, and nurtured as lifelong followers of Jesus.

"Why isn't discipleship working like it used to?" Perhaps because we have been firing away at the wrong target. Instead of being concerned primarily about students' attendance and knowledge, we would be better off if we centered our attention on the essence of discipling adolescents for the long haul—in a world that has abandoned them, the church is their home.

DEEP DESIGN PROMPT

STEP 1: NOW?   STEP 3: WHO?

STEP 4: HOW?   STEP 2: NEW?

DEEP DESIGN, STEP 3 (OBSERVATION): *WHO?*

Chuck Neder has been in youth ministry for 40 years (no kidding!), the last 30 as executive director and now CEO of Fun in the Son Ministries.[20] This organization provides conferences, camps, service opportunities, training for youth leaders, and parenting seminars for churches. Chuck has influenced youth work in the church, especially the Presbyterian Church, through his direct work with students as well as his preaching and teaching. He also has taken a careful and deliberate look at the goal of youth ministry, considering how it needs to change in both the ministry he leads and youth ministry at large. I had a chance to ask Chuck some important questions:

Chuck, what was the goal when you began your career in youth ministry?

To get and keep a job and to get a lot of kids to come to my events. The way we evaluated ourselves was how many kids came to our events. In the 1970s we didn't talk a lot about discipleship. The goal was to pack as much information into them as we could and then follow up on that by watching their behavior. We would counsel them to "do" the faith, which meant encouraging them to have daily quiet times and quit drinking. That was all that mattered.

How has that goal changed for you?

Over the last several years I have come to realize that what we had been teaching kids about the Christian faith was more about the outside than the inside. I never talked about the journey of faith or suffering or finding your identity by being a member of God's diverse family. I wanted them to *look* like good "Christians" who *behaved* like people

---

[20] Formerly known as PFR Youth Ministry (Presbyterians for Renewal).

DEEP MINISTRY

I could point to and say, "Hey, they're my disciples." I knew they actually were Jesus' disciples, but I felt like I was the one who had somehow made their compliance happen while they were in my ministry.

What are some of the consequences of poor understandings of the goal of youth ministry?

I now believe that for the last several decades we have failed kids. We have taught them to trust in a gospel that isn't even true, one that says, "Do the right things, follow these steps, memorize these words, and your life will turn out great, God will bless you." Not that God *won't* bless, but what that blessing looks like was not part of the package I presented. I wanted to entice kids to trust a God that would never let them suffer or hurt. But Hebrews 5:8 says that Jesus "learned obedience from what he suffered." I now realize that I robbed kids of the deep mystery of the gospel by offering an external, performance-oriented Christianity.

What type of relationship should youth ministries have with the overall church?

I used to think youth ministry was all a kid needed. But I have come to see that we all need one another, young and old alike, to experience what God has for us. I also led kids to "become Christians," meaning that they said a prayer and practiced some of the disciplines. But now I see that the disciplines are tools to get to something deeper—an intimacy with Christ and his body. It is not the job, then, of youth ministry to "make disciples," it is the job of the church. Youth ministry helps provide a bridge into the body that becomes a discipling community throughout their lives.

What is the goal of your conferences? Your mission trips? Your youth worker training events?

I have also seen kids change over the last several years. It used to be that when we gave them great music and solid teaching, they responded. That doesn't seem so much the case anymore. They have become more distant, wounded by what society has done to them, and therefore they are less able to trust us. In our conferences and mission trips, we are counselor-centered, meaning that we rely on the ongoing relationships of leaders with students to build the trust that sets the stage for our programs. In training youth workers, we remind them that their first job is to make sure kids know they care—before they try to do anything "spiritual" with them.

If you were to give one bit of advice to today's student ministry leaders, what would it be?

Let Jesus have his way with you, embrace and learn from the suffering that is inevitable in a fallen world, and help kids see that they are part of God's family *now*, with gifts and talents the entire church needs. If you never give up working on your own soul, pursuing honesty and depth, then what you offer kids will be real and attractive. And never forget that the church, with all its faults, is what God set up to carry his message across the ages.

DEEP DESIGN, STEP 4 (APPLICATION): *HOW?*

Application Questions:

DEEP DESIGN PROMPT

STEP 1: NOW?   STEP 3: WHO?

STEP 4: HOW?   STEP 2: NEW?

1. What has been your goal in your ministry program? In light of this chapter, do you feel like your goal lines up with Jesus' Great Commission in Matthew 28:18-20?

2. What does it mean for you to have a target that sends you to "all the nations"? Name two or three ways that would change what you are doing now.

3. How well does your program promote assimilating students into the larger body of Christ? Do you have a specific transitional strategy to help your students move from being treated like kids (and acting like kids) into full discipleship and fellowship within the community of faith? What is one way you could strengthen this aspect of your ministry?

4. If the baptism or dedication service for your church includes vows that are affirmed by the congregation, get a copy of these vows and ask: *How does what I do encourage what the church promises?* Even if your church does not have such rituals, in what ways does your program encourage students to become functioning and emotionally connected members of the church family? In what ways does it keep them from being connected to the overall body?

5. On a scale of 1 to 7 (7 being the most effective), how effective is your program in producing disciples who obey "everything" Jesus taught? (Hint: if you're not sure what this means, spend some time studying Matthew 5-7, a great passage summarizing Jesus' teaching.)

6. How is your ministry perspective similar to Chuck Neder's? How is your perspective different?

DEEP MINISTRY

7. How will you go deeper in your understanding of the goal of youth ministry?

How are we going to go deeper in our ministry goal(s)?	Source

SECTION 2
DEEPER WITH PEOPLE

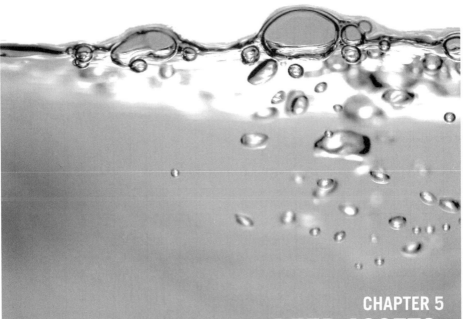

CHAPTER 5

DEEP ASSETS: WHAT BESIDES "YOUTH MINISTRY" DOES A KID NEED TO *REALLY* GROW?

Kara Powell

∞ **DEEP DESIGN PROMPT**

Creating Space for God's transformation: Kids are excited about Jesus.

∞ **DEEP DESIGN PROMPT**

Hindering God's transformation: Obstacles that prevent students from developing.

DEEP DESIGN, STEP 1 (DISCERNMENT): *NOW?*

"Kara, I'm tired of loving kids in my ministry and then sending them right back to hell."

I knew Rodney well enough to know *hell* was not a word he used lightly. I asked this veteran youth worker what he meant.

"Kids are all excited about Jesus when they're around me, but so many of them have terrible situations at home. How deep can I take them in the two hours I have them every week?"

I knew immediately what he was talking about. I thought of Alia, a sophomore whose parents were too addicted to drugs to raise her, so they sent her to live with her aunt and uncle.

I also thought of Scott. Captain of the soccer team, popular at school and church, at the top of his class academically—Scott seemed to have it all together. But underneath the applause was a 17-year-old scared of what would happen at home if he let down his dad.

Of course, along with kids like Alia and Scott are many students who walk out of our youth gatherings and into families that pay attention to them, support them, and make sacrifices for their well being. Yet even in these promising homes, it's impossible for family members to always love and serve kids in the right ways at the right times. How can we have deep ministry with kids when they live in communities and families that struggle and sometimes even undermine our work with them?

Is Jesus Enough?

Here are a few questions to get you thinking: *True or False? Kids need Jesus.*

If you've spent the money to buy this book and the time to read it, you're probably someone who follows Jesus and wants your kids to follow him as well. As I've heard many youth workers teach, a relationship with Jesus establishes a "foundation" for everything else.

Here's a second question: *True or False? Jesus is all that kids need.*

At first, this seems like an easy one. True, right? We've sung words such as, "Your love is all that I need" and "All I need is you." But what about the inner-city sophomore who's being raised by his older sister and can't read? He needs Jesus plus some literacy training. Or how about the girl whose parents just told her they're getting divorced? She needs Jesus, and she also may need some counseling.

A common problem in youth ministry **Now** is that we've taken the true statement that "kids need Jesus" and left out the other things kids need that don't seem so spiritual. Sure, most of us agree that Jesus is the foundation. But many kids living in hellish home situations will continue to struggle unless we also provide a few walls and a roof to support their growth.

Support Wall #1: Adult mentors. Lots of youth ministries recognize that while Jesus may be the foundation, kids also need adult mentors and disciplers. Sometimes these adults "float" through the ministry, keeping an eye out for kids who need extra attention. Other ministries assign certain adults to certain kids to make sure that every student gets attention from at least one adult. (See Chapter 6 for more on adult mentoring.)

Support Wall #2: Educational help. Common in urban ministries, this second wall often comes in the form of after-school tutoring, computer centers, and aid in filling out college applications. Since this type of academic

 **DEEP DESIGN PROMPT**

Hindering God's transformation: We focus only on "spiritual" needs.

 **DEEP DESIGN PROMPT**

Creating space for God's transformation: Adults who build relationships with kids.

DEEP DESIGN PROMPT

Creating space for God's transformation: Educational help.

help generally involves working closely with an adult, it reinforces the first wall of adult mentoring. As one youth worker who had integrated a tutoring center into his church told me, "If a kid can't read, it's the church's job to help that kid learn to read."

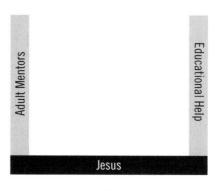

5.1

DEEP DESIGN PROMPT

Hindering God's transformation: A couple of walls do not make a strong house.

Given kids' vast and varied needs, these two walls are important in helping kids and adults flesh out what it means to have Jesus as the foundation. But if you've ever tried building a house of cards, you know two walls alone don't offer much stability. Without a roof, the walls take a beating when it rains. Strong winds can toss those walls to the ground. None of us would choose to live in a house with only two walls, and yet that's often how we structure our ministries. As a result, kids end up too shallow to stand against the storms that come their way.

DEEP DESIGN PROMPT

STEP 1: NOW?   STEP 3: WHO?

STEP 4: HOW?   STEP 2: NEW?

DEEP DESIGN, STEP 2 (REFLECTION): *NEW?*

Recent research shows us a deeper approach to ministering to kids that's more holistic than simply adding adults and tutoring into their lives. Instead of just two walls, kids need **New** "scaffolding."

Scaffolding is a social science term to describe the importance of social interaction in a child's development. Adults who interact with kids in warm and challenging ways provide the support that helps kids really learn and grow. Just as with buildings under construction, scaffolding is also crucial during child and adolescent development. As teenagers mature and grow more independent and capable, the scaffolding can be reduced.

∞ DEEP DESIGN PROMPT

Research: Kids need scaffolding.

While the term *scaffolding* isn't in the Bible, the concept certainly is. Christians today often view "family" through a narrow lens, equating it with a nuclear family of parents and children. In reality "family" extends far beyond an "us four and no more" focus. When Jesus came, he ushered in both a new kingdom and a new family. All who do the will of the divine Father are our brothers and sisters in this **New** family (Mark 3:31-34).

∞ DEEP DESIGN PROMPT

Scripture: Jesus brings a broad sense of family that includes all who serve the divine Father.

A NARROW VIEW OF FAMILY

A BROAD VIEW OF FAMILY

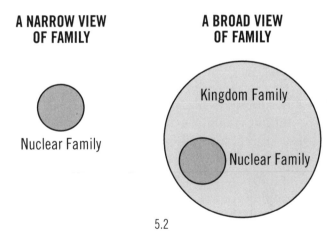

5.2

Jesus confirms this **New** sense of family in his dying words to his mother. As Mary watches her son's agonizing crucifixion, Jesus tells her, "Dear woman, here is your son" (John 19:26). Jesus then turns to the disciple (presumably

John) and says, "Here is your mother" (John 19:27a). John records next that "from that time on, this disciple took her into his home" (John 19:27b). Jesus establishes a **New** mother/son relationship not based on traditional blood ties but on the ties that come from the blood he shed on the cross.[21]

More than two millennia later, we have the opportunity to reveal this deeper sense of family to the world. Jesus has invited us to join the **New** kingdom family, and now we can continue his work and invite others to join also (John 14:12). Jesus did more than just teach about "spiritual" needs; he healed, fed, and cared about how people treated one another. Just as Jesus offered more than his words (Luke 4:18-19), so we now offer more than our verbal witness to others. In a sense, we are Jesus' loving hands to those inside and outside the divine family, embodying the caring scaffolding that kids and families need (Matthew 5:3-10; Luke 10:25-28; 1 Corinthians 13:1-13; 1 John 4:7-8).

The Importance of Assets

The Search Institute, a well-known research center in Minnesota, helps us use this **New** type of scaffolding to allow our ministries to go deeper. Based on surveys with more than two million youth in the United States and Canada since 1989, Search has developed the "40 Developmental Assets"—40 building blocks of development available through our surrounding communities and relationships that help people of all ages (including teenagers) thrive. Half the assets are "external" and focus on what kids receive from others. They fall under the categories of support, empowerment, boundaries and expectations, and constructive use of time. The remaining half of the assets are "internal" and reflect the four constructs of commitment to learning, positive values, social competencies, and positive identity.[22]

[21] Rodney Clapp, *Families at the Crossroads* (Downers Grove, Illinois: Inter Varsity Press, 1993), 81.

[22] To peruse more asset-based resources developed by Search Institute, go to www.search-institute.org. You could also check out Peter Benson, *All Kids Are Our Kids: What Communities Must Do to Raise Caring and Responsible Children and Adolescents* (San Francisco: Jossey-Bass, 1997).

40 DEVELOPMENTAL ASSETS FROM SEARCH INSTITUTE

EXTERNAL ASSETS

CATEGORY	ASSET NAME AND DEFINITION
SUPPORT	1. Family support – Family life provides high levels of love and support.
	2. Positive family communication – Young person and her or his parent(s) communicate positively, and young person is willing to seek advice and counsel from parents.
	3. Other adult relationships – Young person receives support from three or more nonparent adults.
	4. Caring neighborhood – Young person experiences caring neighbors.
	5. Caring school climate – School provides a caring, encouraging environment.
	6. Parent involvement in schooling – parent(s) are actively involved in helping young person succeed in school.
EMPOWERMENT	7. Community values youth – Young person perceives that adults in the community value youth.
	8. Youth as resources – Young people are given useful roles in the community.
	9. Service to others – Young person serves in the community one hour or more per week.
	10. Safety – Young person feels safe at home, school, and in the neighborhood.
BOUNDARIES & EXPECTATIONS	11. Family boundaries – Family has clear rules and consequences and monitors the young person's whereabouts.
	12. School boundaries – School provides clear rules and consequences.
	13. Neighborhood boundaries – Neighbors take responsibility for monitoring young people's behavior.
	14. Adult role models – Parent(s) and other adults model positive, responsible behavior.
	15. Positive peer influence – Young person's best friends model responsible behavior.
	16. High expectations – Both parent(s) and teachers encourage the young person to do well.
CONSTRUCTIVE USE OF TIME	17. Creative activities – Young person spends three or more hours per week in lessons or practice in music, theatre, or other arts.
	18. Youth programs – Young person spends three or more hours per week in sports, clubs, or organizations at school and/or in the community.
	19. Religious community – Young person spends one or more hours per week in activities in religious institutions.
	20. Time at home – Young person is out with friends "with nothing special to do" two or fewer nights per week.

5.3

INTERNAL ASSETS

CATEGORY	ASSET NAME AND DEFINITION
COMMITMENT TO LEARNING	21. Achievement motivation – Young person is motivated to do well in school.
	22. School engagement – Young person is actively engaged in learning.
	23. Homework – Young person reports doing at least one hour of homework every school day.
	24. Bonding to school – Young person cares about her or his school.
	25. Reading for pleasure – Young person reads for pleasure three or more hours per week.
POSITIVE VALUES	26. Caring – Young person places high value on helping other people.
	27. Equality and social justice – Young person places high value on promoting equality and reducing hunger and poverty.
	28. Integrity – Young person acts on convictions and stands up for her or his beliefs.
	29. Honesty – Young person "tells the truth even when it is not easy."
	30. Responsibility – Young person accepts and takes personal responsibility.
	31. Restraint – Young person believes it is important not to be sexually active or to use alcohol or other drugs.
SOCIAL COMPETENCIES	32. Planning and decision-making – Young person knows how to plan ahead and make choices.
	33. Interpersonal competence – Young person has empathy, sensitivity, and friendship skills.
	34. Cultural competence – Young person has knowledge of and comfort with people of different cultural/racial/ethnic backgrounds.
	35. Resistance skills – Young person can resist negative peer pressure and dangerous situations.
	36. Peaceful conflict resolution – Young person seeks to resolve conflict nonviolently.
POSITIVE IDENTITY	37. Personal power – Young person feels he or she has control over "things that happen to me."
	38. Self-esteem – Young person reports having a high self-esteem.
	39. Sense of purpose – Young person reports that "my life has a purpose."
	40. Positive view of personal future – Young person is optimistic about his or her personal future.

For more information, see www.search-institute.org.

5.4

We who long for deep ministry must pay attention to these assets and their power in kids' lives. Research indicates that the more assets kids possess, the more likely they are to exhibit leadership, maintain good health, value diversity, and succeed in school. In contrast, the fewer assets kids possess, the more likely they are to use alcohol and drugs, be sexually active, and commit acts of violence.

> **∞ DEEP DESIGN PROMPT**
> Research: The more assets kids possess, the better they do.

The average 6th to 12th-grader Search surveyed has 19.3 of the 40 assets. In general, older youth have lower average levels of assets than younger youth. Interestingly, boys seem to experience fewer assets than girls.

Although there is no "magic number" of assets that guarantees kids will thrive, Search hints that 31 assets is a common benchmark that divides kids who do well from those who struggle. Only nine percent of the youth they've surveyed have 31 or more assets. Assets evident in 30 percent or less of the youth they've surveyed include the following:

> **∞ DEEP DESIGN PROMPT**
> Research: Most kids do not have enough assets.

- Positive family communication (asset 2)

- Caring school climate (asset 5)

- Community values youth (asset 7)

- Youth as resources (asset 8)

- Adult role models (asset 14)

- Creative activities (asset 17)

- Reading for pleasure (asset 25)

- Planning and decision-making (asset 32)

Search Institute also reports that many of the assets are evident in 60 percent or more of the youth they surveyed including these:

- Family support (asset 1)

- Positive peer influence (asset 15)

- Religious community (asset 19)

- Achievement motivation (asset 21)

- School engagement (asset 22)

- Integrity (asset 28)

- Honesty (asset 29)

- Responsibility (asset 30)

- Positive view of personal future (asset 40)

Much of what we've typically valued in youth ministry is represented in the 40 assets. Relationship with Jesus and involvement in church is relevant to asset 19 of religious community, which means a kid spends one or more hours per week in activities in a religious institution. Our first "support wall" of adult mentoring is specifically represented in asset 14 of "adult role models." Similarly, our second support wall of educational help is connected to school engagement (asset 22) and doing at least one hour of homework every school day (asset 23).

DEEP DESIGN PROMPT

Research: Many youth ministries don't intentionally offer the assets.

Yet other assets exist that many youth ministries don't even consider as they try to love and serve kids. These include a caring neighborhood (asset 4), caring school climate (asset 5), creative activities (asset 17), cultural competence (asset 34), and peaceful conflict resolution (asset 36). Helping kids out of their "hellish" homes, schools, and neighborhoods—or even just helping them through the common ups and downs of adolescence—means we need to think about how we provide not just a few walls or a few assets but an entire **New** structure of support.

DEEP MINISTRY

DEEP DESIGN, STEP 3 (OBSERVATION): *WHO?*

∞ DEEP DESIGN PROMPT

STEP 1: NOW?   STEP 3: WHO?

STEP 4: HOW?   STEP 2: NEW?

Curt Gibson, the Neighborhood Student Mentoring Director at Lake Avenue Church in Pasadena, California, is trying to help kids develop a stronger scaffolding of support. He found the 40 developmental assets so relevant to his kids and community that he placed them at the heart of his ministry. We interviewed Curt to discover how the assets influence his ministry and how they might be relevant to you and your ministry.

How did you first become interested in the assets?

I heard about them at a conference and decided to do a little experiment in our ministry. One student we were just getting to know was Kamesha. She was living in northwest Pasadena with her brother, sister, cousin, mom, and grandma—all in a one-bedroom apartment.

How'd you start with Kamesha?

First, we got to know her mom better and told her about the assets. Then we met with Kamesha's teachers at her continuation school. We also explained the assets to them and asked them to give Kamesha's mom progress reports three times a semester.

We met with Kamesha's neighbors in her 19-unit apartment complex. We introduced ourselves, explained the assets and the importance of a friendly neighborhood, and asked them to talk to Kamesha and become her friend. Kamesha hated that.

Why did she hate it?

She had been intimidating all of her neighbors and misbehaving around the empty swimming pool in the middle of the apartments. That got harder to do once she had actually met her neighbors.

We also met with her pastor—or rather the pastor at her grandma's church. Kamesha told the pastor why she hated the church so much, and he took it like a pro. He listened to her, validated what she said, and then asked, "What would this church need to be like for you and your friends to want to come here?" Plus, he asked her what she liked to do, and she said she liked music. Soon after that, he asked her to be in charge of their seven-member youth choir and praise dance team.

What kind of difference did establishing a better connection with her mom, teachers, neighbors, and church make for Kamesha?

Huge changes. She started actually coming to school. There was one particular teacher whom she worked especially hard for, even to the point of going to the library to use the free computer so she could type out her assignments. She started getting to know her neighbors and smiling at them instead of ignoring them or intimidating them.

So having gone through an experiment with Kamesha, what did you do next?

Given how well it worked with her, we decided to make the assets the foundation of all we do. We're doing more and more mentoring (asset 14). We now have 17 mentors, each working with two or three kids.

Plus, since the assets recommend that kids have fewer than three nights per week with nothing to do, we need to get kids off the street and keep them busy. We signed one guy up for karate, and we paid for a girl to join a basketball league. We bought kids guitars and trumpets and paid for music lessons. Of course, that meant we had to put our money where our mouth is, because that stuff costs money.

We also started working differently with kids' parents. It was a huge step for us to talk with them and explain the assets and what we were trying to do with their kids. But then we did even more than that. We tried to connect parents with current services in the city so they could get the support they needed, whether it be legal advice, jobs, or even help feeding their kids healthy meals.

So you connected parents to resources?

Yes, in fact that's become a mantra of our ministry. I tell our mentors that instead of trying to *be* the resource for their kids, they should *find* the resources for their kids.

What assets are most of your kids missing, and what assets do they tend to have?

They're almost universally missing a community that values youth (asset 7) and a positive view of personal future (asset 40).

In terms of assets they tend to have, I'd say caring school climate (asset 5) and youth programs (asset 18), because of all the nonprofits in the city of Pasadena.

To see the Youth Inventory Assessment and Goal worksheet Curt's adult leaders use to reflect upon the assets with their own kids, check out www.cyfm.net.

Which assets seem to produce the deepest changes in kids?

The three that we've found that have great effect and are pretty do-able are adult role models (asset 14), religious community (asset 19), and time at home (asset 20). Others that are super powerful but harder to accomplish are personal power, self-esteem, sense of purpose, and a positive view of personal future (assets 37-40).

What are some obstacles you've faced in trying to have an asset-focused ministry?

See chapter 6 on mentoring for more on "sin management."

See chapter 6 for more on the challenges of mentoring.

Well, some people who volunteer as mentors basically just want to lead a Bible study. I'm all for Bible studies, but this is different. This is a deeper view of the kingdom of God that says following Jesus means more than sin management.

It says that the kingdom of God means we're active in trying to serve and improve families, schools, and the entire community. Lots of volunteers don't get that, and quite honestly, they leave.

It also takes a lot of adult volunteers to be this involved in kids' lives. We try to have one adult for every two kids, and that means we need a lot of adults.

Plus, it often takes at least three months before an adult gets any sort of positive response from these kids. Lots of adults can't cut it and drop out. That means that the next mentor has to wait even longer before those same kids start responding.

What mistakes did you make when you were first trying to do ministry in this way?

Our biggest mistake was that we didn't teach the theological perspective of the kingdom of God that says we are to engage in our communities. So many people equate following Jesus only with doing Bible studies. I think that's a truncated Jesus. Now I ask potential volunteers to read the first few chapters of *The Divine Conspiracy* to help them get what we're doing.

To see the Personal Mission Statement worksheet that Curt and his team uses, go to www.cyfm.net.

We also set intermediate goals for kids now. We used to get so bummed when kids would hang out with us and still be in gangs. The reality is that it often takes years for kids to realize the emptiness of the activities they've done for so long. We try to have goals for kids that are based more on values and heart change than external behaviors.

We also involve kids in thinking more about their own lives. We teach them about personal mission statements and then have them create one and share it with their adult mentor. That way adults and kids are talking about where the kids want to head, and how they can take baby steps to get there. We have kids who want to be pediatricians, but they never go to class. They don't see that disconnect until we start asking them if they're headed in the right direction to reach their goals.

What advice would you give to someone who wants to do asset-based youth ministry?

If you're already in a ministry, you might need to shut it down and rebuild from a kingdom perspective that focuses more on community than programs. If you or your ministry supervisor care about how fast your group grows, this is not the model for you. This is more about personal growth than numerical growth.

We also interviewed Stephanie Moore who serves with Curt at Neighborhood Student Mentoring. She finds the assets offer "a great foundation" to help kids thrive. Stephanie is currently mentoring two high-risk girls. She focuses on helping them realize the community values them (asset 7), integrating them into a religious community (asset 19), and giving them some structured activities at night (asset 20).

Yet she cautioned that, even with the assets guiding her, it took six months of hanging out with her girls before they started responding positively to her. She recalls, "They used to make fun of me and only want to be with me because I'd give them a ride somewhere or take them out to eat. I *so* wanted to quit, but I hung in there. After six months they finally seemed to care about me as more than a chauffeur."

It's not like her girls have completely left their old lifestyles, she said. They still do drugs and drink periodically. But Stephanie is encouraged that now "they actually *want* to spend time with me." They also do their homework now, and have a good chance at graduating from high school. Before their interactions with Stephanie and the assets, these all seemed like impossibilities.

DEEP DESIGN, STEP 4 (APPLICATION): *HOW?*

∞ DEEP DESIGN PROMPT

STEP 1: NOW?   STEP 3: WHO?

STEP 4: HOW?   STEP 2: NEW?

Application Questions:

1. What kinds of "hell" do the kids in your ministry face?

2. When you think of "family," do you think of a biological family, a kingdom family, or both? How does your view of family affect how you relate to others?

3. Look at the list of the assets on pages 95 and 96. Which ones do your kids tend to possess?

4. Which assets do your youth tend to lack?

5. Which assets do you think would be most likely to produce changes in the lives of your youth?

6. How do you feel about Curt's statement that instead of "trying to be the resource for their kids, they should find the resources for their kids"?

7. What about your ministry is similar to Curt's? How is your ministry different?

8. How will you go deeper in holistic ministry with your kids?

How are we going to go deeper in our ministrywith kids?	Source

CHAPTER 6

DEEP MENTORS: WHY AREN'T OUR MENTORS GETTING AS DEEP AS WE'D LIKE?

Kara Powell

DEEP DESIGN, STEP 1 (DISCERNMENT): *NOW?*

I've become a soccer mom.

Nathan, our oldest, is four years old and now eligible to play soccer. He loves soccer. Actually, he loves kicking pretty much any type of ball. Baseballs, tennis balls, volleyballs—it doesn't matter to him. Anything that's round and rolls, he tries to kick. So soccer seemed like a logical sport for him.

The day I went to register with the American Youth Soccer Organization, they asked if I would volunteer to help coach his team. I don't have much soccer experience, but these are four year olds. How hard can it be?

So I asked how many hours it would take.

Twenty.

Twenty hours of training. Seriously?

Twenty hours of training to teach four year olds how to kick a soccer ball into a net. Sure, there are a few funky rules—such as what it means to be offsides and whether a penalty merits a direct or an indirect kick. But basically we're talking four year olds and a soccer ball.

How many hours of training have you received this year to do youth ministry? Two hours? Eight hours? Maybe even 15 hours? If so, you're doing pretty well. Probably even better than average.

It's not that the AYSO has it wrong. I think they've got it right—and we in the church should take some notes. In youth ministry **Now**, we ask adults to live out the kingdom before teenagers, but we give them only a fraction of the training our culture gives those who teach children how to kick soccer balls.

∞ DEEP DESIGN PROMPT

Hindering God's transformation: We don't invest enough in training.

I know one youth worker who wished she had more training before she started hanging out with kids. In her first five years as a youth worker, she sailed through three different definitions of mentoring. Her first was quite simple: *toiletpapering*. A firm convert to relational ministry, she figured the best way to spend time with kids was to do whatever they wanted. And there was only one thing her freshman girls wanted to do: go toiletpapering. In the midst of the planning, driving, toiletpapering, and giggling—lots of giggling—the youth worker felt she was building valuable friendships with the girls.

But after a few years of toiletpapering, she began sensing that her mentoring wasn't deep enough. There was lots of laughter and lots of talking, but not much real or personal sharing.

So she moved to her second definition of mentoring: *frozen yogurt with a question about God*. As long as her girls had a few spoonfuls of God over a few spoonfuls of yogurt, she felt she was really mentoring them.

While that gave the relationships more depth, after a few years she still felt she was splashing in the shallow end. She figured the only way to dive into the deep end was through her new, third definition of mentoring: *telling kids what to do*. What kids needed was guidance, and she was going to dole it out.

In your own past or present as a youth worker, can you relate to any of these definitions of mentoring? All three sound very familiar to me.

That's because the youth worker I've been describing is me.

Part of me wishes I could go back to the kids I "mentored" in those early phases and ask them for a do-over. Sure, relationships were built, and sure, God worked. But

∞ **DEEP DESIGN PROMPT**

Creating space for God's transformation: Youth workers recognizing the power of building relationships with kids.

∞ **DEEP DESIGN PROMPT**

Hindering God's transformation: Often in the midst of the "fun," we never get deep.

∞ **DEEP DESIGN PROMPT**

Creating space for God's transformation: Asking a few questions about God when we're with students.

∞ **DEEP DESIGN PROMPT**

Hindering God's transformation: Maybe a few questions about God aren't enough.

∞ DEEP DESIGN PROMPT

Creating space for God's transformation: Working in the midst of our flawed mentoring.

∞ DEEP DESIGN PROMPT

Creating space for God's transformation: More ministries are integrating mentoring into their strategies.

my poor definitions of mentoring were like Water Wings around our relational ministry that kept us from swimming deeper.

My current definition of mentoring is *empowering others toward God's purposes for their lives.*[23] Note the absence of toilet paper, frozen yogurt, or lectures. It's no wonder that mentoring is all the rage in youth ministry **Now**. More and more youth workers are realizing the value of mentoring in helping kids fall deeply in love with Jesus. Whether it takes the form of one-on-one relationships or small groups, mentoring is becoming an integral part of urban, suburban, rural, and international ministries.

Nonetheless, we've **Now** bought into a number of myths about mentoring that keep us shallow. Without spending a lot more time and energy in our mentoring relationships, are there elements we could be incorporating that would produce more intimate relationships? In order to move into deep relationships, what myths about mentoring do we need to toss overboard?

∞ DEEP DESIGN PROMPT

STEP 1: NOW?   STEP 3: WHO?

STEP 4: HOW?   **STEP 2: NEW?**

DEEP DESIGN, STEP 2 (REFLECTION): *NEW?*

Myths about Mentoring That Keep Us Shallow

Myth 1: Something is better than nothing.

When I was a college student and a junior high volunteer, our team leader tried to encourage us by saying that when it came to building relationships with kids, "Something is better than nothing." As a hard-working college student trying to squeeze in time with junior highers between classes, homework, and hanging out with friends in the dorm, his words made me feel much better about the crumbs of time I gave kids. He made our whole team feel better. After all, we were busy students, stay-at-home

---

[23] Paul Stanley and J. Robert Clinton, *Connecting* (Colorado Springs, CO: NavPress, 1992), 33.

parents, or business leaders. We couldn't give much time to mentoring relationships with kids, but that was okay. Something was better than nothing.

I wish that were the case. I really do. But **New** research tells us it's not always true. Sometimes something is actually *worse* than nothing.

∞ DEEP DESIGN PROMPT

Experience: We often give kids scraps of time and energy.

There's a surprising scarcity of actual research on youth mentoring, especially when you consider how widely it's practiced in church, parachurch, and secular youth organizations. But one of the consistent findings is that relationships are most effective when two things happen:

1. The adult and the youth meet for at least 10 hours per month,[24] and

2. They meet for at least 12 months.

Secular research has examined the effects of mentoring on high-risk students' self-worth, family relationships, drug and alcohol abstinence, school attendance and performance, and positive social behaviors. The good news is that all these tend to improve if an adult meets regularly with a kid for a year or more. But now comes the bad news: if adults meet with troubled kids for less than six months, these kids tend to have *lower* rates of drug and alcohol abstinence, school attendance and performance, and positive social behaviors.[25]

∞ DEEP DESIGN PROMPT

Research: Sometimes those scraps actually damage kids.

While the researchers don't suggest any reasons why a truncated mentoring relationship actually harms kids, it may connect with what we've already discussed in Chapter 4 on discipleship. To kids who already feel abandoned by adults, a mentor who severs a relationship is just one more adult who walks out on them.

That theory resonates with other research findings. The negative effects of a short mentoring relationship are even

---

[24] C. Herrera, L. Sipe, and W.S. McClanahan, *Mentoring School Age Children: Relationship Development in Community-Based and School-Based Programs* (Philadelphia: Public/Private Ventures, 2000).
[25] Jean Rhodes, *Stand By Me: The Risks and Rewards of Mentoring Today's Youth* (Cambridge: Harvard University Press, 2002), 60.

more severe if the teenager highly values the relationship.[26] If kids take the time to build trusting relationships with adults, and then for some reason those relationships fade away, kids are even more likely to engage in antisocial behaviors and have greater difficulty in school.

∞ DEEP DESIGN PROMPT

Research: We need high expectations for our mentors. We can't "settle" for less.

While these **New** findings relate specifically to higher-risk youth, they are relevant to youth in any social situation. No matter what kinds of kids we're spending time with, we have to consider what kind of damage we might be doing if we don't meet with them regularly, or if we decide to end the mentoring relationships before they expect it. Adults who want to be mentors or small group leaders should ask themselves: "Can I do this for 12 months, and can I give close to 10 hours each month?" If not, then they should wait until they can.

∞ DEEP DESIGN PROMPT

Scripture: Jesus modeled long-term depth with those he most closely mentored.

The power of such long-term commitment is illustrated in Jesus' relationships with those he closely mentored—his disciples. The scribes and religious teachers of Jesus' day generally trained their followers through formal teaching and mandatory rituals. Jesus' strategy was different: he was with his followers day and night and talked about what they experienced together. The essence of Jesus' mentoring ministry was hanging out, and hanging out for a while (Mark 3:14).

∞ DEEP DESIGN PROMPT

History: Mentoring takes longer when our goal is to change not only external behaviors but also internal beliefs.

Why did Jesus spend so much time with his disciples 2,000 years ago? And why does it take so long for mentoring relationships to change kids' lives today? Because true mentoring means changing not just external behaviors, but also internal perspectives. Dallas Willard writes, "One of the greatest weaknesses in our teaching and leadership today is that we spend so much time trying to get people to do things good people are supposed to do, without changing what they really believe."[27] Commenting specifically about youth, Willard continues, "We frankly need to do

[26] Ibid, 59.
[27] Dallas Willard, *The Divine Conspiracy* (New York: Harper Collins Publisher, 1998), 307.

much less of this managing of action, especially with young people. We need to concentrate on changing the minds of those we would reach and serve."[28]

Longevity in mentoring is important because the beliefs we need to change aren't merely those that are secondary to our faith. Willard proposes that our transformation of beliefs must start with the most central component of our faith: the gospel. In the theological spectrum of Christian proclamation and practice over the last century, two extremes have developed. According to Willard, right-wing (or more "conservative") theology has focused on forgiveness of the *individual's* sins; left-wing (or more "liberal") theology has emphasized the removal of social and societal evils. Willard suggests that these are both examples of the "gospel of sin management."[29] Giving students a fresh approach to the gospel that includes both of these elements under a larger rubric of God's work in the world through his people cannot be accomplished overnight. That type of deep belief and life transformation requires more than drive-by mentoring.

> ∞ **DEEP DESIGN PROMPT**
>
> History: Too many of us have reduced the "good news" to the "gospel of sin management."[29]

Myth 2: Once you recruit adult mentors, your work is done.

We often think the hardest part of connecting adults to kids is finding the adults who want to be connected to kids. We spend months beating the bushes, asking others we know, placing appeals in church and ministry newsletters, recruiting, and praying that God will send workers for the ripe harvest. When he brings workers our way, we meet with them for coffee and answer any questions they might have. Then we connect them with a few students and chalk up another effective mentoring relationship for our ministry.

> ∞ **DEEP DESIGN PROMPT**
>
> Experience: We often think most of our work is done once we match up students and adults.

Not so fast.

[28] Ibid.
[29] Ibid, 41.

I wish mentoring were as easy as pairing people up and then letting them march into mentoring heaven. But research tells us otherwise. **New** findings tell us that recruiting is just the first step in the journey of learning and growth.

There are three steps that seem to contribute to deeper mentoring relationships that may not be part of your current ministry.[30]

∞ DEEP DESIGN PROMPT

Research: We need to conduct a thorough screening of our potential mentors.

1. Proper Screening. Sure, an adult seems nice and has the right answers when you ask him why he wants to mentor kids. But do you really know him? Can you really trust him?

As I tell youth workers in seminars, "If you want to molest kids, volunteer in churches." Jaws tend to drop, so I continue. "Youth ministries are terrible at making sure the adults we send out for pizza with kids, or even on overnighters, are really out for kids' best interests."

When you meet with volunteers to explain their potential roles in your ministry, view it not as a sales pitch but as an interview. Your goal is to see whether or not they are *worthy* to hang out with kids. It's not to convince them to get involved, but to see if they pass the high bar of mentoring kids. That means you ask them questions about their journeys with God, past relationships, and temptations they struggle with.

In addition, please check with two to three of their references. Ask questions about the potential volunteer's relationship with God, relationships with others, and moral behaviors. Some ministries have even decided to partner with local police stations and conduct fingerprint screening to make sure volunteers don't have criminal records. While some critique this as being anti-community, I ap-

---

[30] Jean Rhodes, ed., *A Critical View of Youth Mentoring: New Directions for Youth Development*, No. 93 (Hoboken, NJ: Jossey-Bass, April 2002), 15.

plaud these efforts. I can't imagine anything more pro-community than making sure we protect kids.

After you've conducted proper screening, **New** research reveals the importance of a second step:

2. Proper Training. In a survey of 700 secular mentoring programs, fewer than half provided volunteers with more than two hours of training. More than a fifth of those programs offered no training. Mentors who received fewer than two hours of training had lower levels of satisfaction with their relationships with kids. The flip side is that those who received six or more hours of training had the highest levels of satisfaction.[31]

∞ DEEP DESIGN PROMPT

Research: The more training, the more happy and effective the mentor.

While there's no guarantee that six hours is the magic amount of proper training time, it does raise a question for anyone who wants a deep youth ministry: *how much training do you offer for mentors? If you're involved in ministry as a mentor, have you received enough training?* If you're not satisfied with the answers to these questions, perhaps it's time to schedule some periodic training so mentors get the skills they need to go deep. (Or maybe hook up with your local soccer team since it seems they've got the goods on training!)

Yet it's not just training that mentors need. They also need a third step.

3. Ongoing supervision and encouragement. According to **New** research, several types of ongoing encouragement and support are meaningful and seem to make mentors more effective:

- Having supervisors check with them regularly to see how the relationships are going and offer perspective.

[31] Rhodes, *Stand By Me*, 64.

- Providing support groups for mentors to gather and problem-solve roadblocks they're facing.

- Probably least practiced by youth ministries is offering small stipends to offset the costs associated with mentoring, such as transportation, baseball game tickets, and meals.[32]

If you lead a team of mentors, how regularly do you check in with each of them? Do you just ask them quickly as you walk past them in the hallway, "Hey, how's it going?" Or are you regularly asking them questions such as *What is going well in your mentoring relationship? What is your greatest struggle? What can I do to help you go deeper?*

If you're not a team leader but are mentoring kids, what can you do to get the support you need? Is there someone you could meet with regularly who could mentor you? Or could you gather a few other mentors for coffee and prayer and commiserating about how tough it can be to care about kids? As you empower kids, you need to be empowered, too.

Myth 3: You can become the "end-all, be-all" mentor.

Wouldn't it be great if our ministries could offer the kind of mentoring Luke Skywalker received in the first *Star Wars* movies? First, he had Obi-Wan Kenobi, who was instrumental in beginning Luke's light saber training and single-handedly freed Luke and his buddies from certain death by sacrificing himself to Darth Vader. Then, Luke gained Yoda as a mentor—a wise Jedi Master whose 900 years of experience were unmatched in the galaxy. What a vast treasure trove of wisdom!

One problem with the *Star Wars* images is that they set up unrealistic expectations for the kind of mentoring we can generally give and receive. Obi-Wan and Yoda were

---

[32] Ibid, 76.

with Luke 24/7. They helped him with everything from lifting starfighters out of swamps to challenges of the will and body.

In his study of mentoring, J. Robert Clinton of Fuller Theological Seminary created a **New** paradigm to help folks receive mentoring in the midst of limited time. Instead of expecting one perfect, all-encompassing mentor, Clinton recommends developing a constellation of mentors, a small galaxy perhaps, of which none is perfect but all can speak into lives.

∞ **DEEP DESIGN PROMPT**

Experience: We wish we were "end-all, be-all" mentors, but we don't have the time and energy.

∞ **DEEP DESIGN PROMPT**

Research: The key is not one mentor, but a small constellation of mentors.

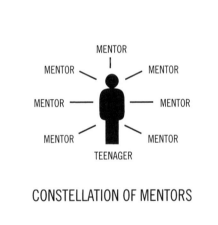

6.1

In his work with Paul D. Stanley, Clinton has grouped the various functions and roles an ideal mentor might perform and placed them along a "continuum of intensity." By thinking of the different roles mentors might play in your youth ministry, you'll have better chances of offering kids the mentoring they need.[33]

---

[33] Figure 6.2 (on page 120) is adapted from Stanley and Clinton, *Connecting: The Mentoring Relationships You Need to Succeed in Life*, 41. The original diagram contains two additional types of mentors: spiritual directors and sponsors.

DEEP DESIGN PROMPT

Research: There are different types of mentors for different needs.

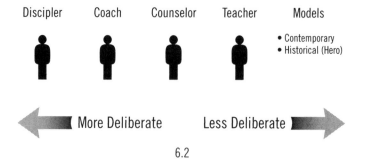

6.2

1. A *discipler* represents a very deliberate relationship that empowers someone in the basics of following Christ. This type of mentoring is crucial for teenagers, especially as they begin their spiritual walks.

2. A *coach* represents a less intensive relationship that gives kids the motivation, skills, and application they need to meet a task or challenge. Common examples of coaches in youth ministry include adults who help kids learn to play a musical instrument, engage in drama, or build a home on a missions trip.

3. A *counselor* provides critical advice and perspective that helps kids navigate their lives and relationships. At times this may even come through professional therapy.

4. A *teacher* helps kids understand how God relates to their lives through discussions, Bible studies, small groups, and one-on-one conversations.

5. A *model* is the least deliberate type of mentoring because it allows any student to receive mentoring by paying attention to others they admire, even if only from a distance.

Recognizing that I have different types of mentoring relationships with different kids has brought great freedom to my ministry. Instead of thinking I need to be every kid's discipler, I've realized there are some kids for whom I am primarily a coach, and others for whom I simply model what it's like to try to follow Jesus when the world makes that difficult.

What about finding mentors for you? If you're interested in learning how to find the mentors you need, check out a free resource at www.cyfm.net.

If you're reading carefully, you might be wondering *Wait a minute! Didn't you say earlier that I might be doing more harm than good if I don't spend 10 hours each month with a kid for the next year? How does that fit with all this talk about different forms of mentoring that call for less time than that?*

The key is what kids expect you to be and do. If they expect you to be a discipler who spends 10 hours a month with them, and you're only planning on coaching them for two hours a month on how to play the guitar, then they'll be disappointed. They'll feel let down and might be more likely to act in ways that reflect their pain.

∞ **DEEP DESIGN PROMPT**

Research: It's important that the adult and student both have the same expectations for their relationship.

But if you both have the same picture of your relationship, then they won't be disappointed. You probably won't have the same deep impact in just a few hours a month that you might if you spent 10 hours, but you can only spend that much time with a handful of kids (which is another reason you need a team—see Chapter 11 on the Superpastor for more on that).

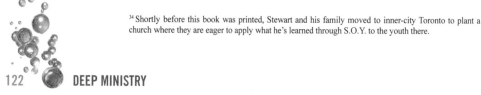
DEEP DESIGN, STEP 3 (OBSERVATION): *WHO?*

Imagine you're a 13-year-old boy, and your dad is abusing your mom and sister. To escape your abusive dad, your mom removes you from your home, your school, and your friends and places you in a shelter facility 30 miles away. You end up dropped into the foster care system with no ties to your former life, no relationships that are constant, and no adult who really knows you.

Except one.

Your mentor.

It was your mentor who heard you say, "I hope you stick with me for the long haul," and then actually did.

When your mom placed you in that shelter, it was your mentor who tracked you down by visiting your mom's former boss and asking for the name of your new city.

It was your mentor who contacted that city's school district to find out the name of your school and then reestablished a relationship with you.

And when you ended up in other foster homes even further away, it was your mentor who drove hours to come and visit you.

This is a true example of the deep impact mentors are having through a ministry in central Iowa called Serve Our Youth (S.O.Y.). For the last five years, executive director Stewart Vander Velden has equipped and expanded a network of congregations to provide high-risk youth with resources and relationships where God's hope and healing are shared.[34] To accomplish that vision, S.O.Y. works with more than 50 Iowa churches from multiple denominations to recruit mentors for kids in detention facilities, jail, shelters, or the foster care system. Regardless of the life situations of the youth you serve, the les-

---

[34] Shortly before this book was printed, Stewart and his family moved to inner-city Toronto to plant a church where they are eager to apply what he's learned through S.O.Y. to the youth there.

sons Stewart has learned in developing a deep mentoring strategy can help your team start discussing how to get out of the shallow end in your own mentoring ministry.

As you think about the hundreds of mentors who've been part of S.O.Y., what does a mentor need to be effective?

The first thing that comes to mind is a sense of commitment. Our best mentors are people who hang with kids through the thick and thin. Kids need mentors who won't get frustrated and walk out on them when they make bad choices. Instead, they need mentors who will believe in them and truly invest in them.

What kind of commitment do you expect of your mentors?

We ask adult mentors to commit to meeting with a kid for one to two hours a week for at least a year. It's the long-term relationships we're after. After meeting for a year, mentors often decide to keep meeting with their kids even though they've fulfilled their initial commitment. They've developed real relationships with their kids, and they don't want to stop meeting.

If someone contacts S.O.Y. and says they want to be a mentor, what type of screening do you do?

Our screening process is pretty extensive. We ask them to complete an application, and then we contact four of their references. We also conduct criminal background checks, sexual offender background checks, driving record checks, child abuse checks, and federal F.B.I. fingerprint background checks. Plus, we do a one-on-one interview. When it comes to matching adults with kids, I don't think you can be too careful.

What kind of training do you offer?

Every mentor receives six hours of training before they are matched with a kid. During that time we describe the qualities of an effective mentor, what we expect of them, and the dos and don'ts of healthy mentoring relationships. We'd rather have our mentors say, "We didn't encounter half of what you told us about" than "You never trained us how to handle that."

How do you match adults with kids?

First, the kid expresses a desire for a mentor. We only assign mentors to kids who say they want to be mentored. Then we try to match mentors by interest. If a kid likes to cook, we try to find a mentor who likes to cook. If a kid likes to fish, we look for an adult who likes to fish. Plus, most of the time we match kids to adults of the same gender. The one exception is if a boy hasn't had much contact with his mom, or if a girl hasn't had much contact with her dad. But even then, our ideal would be to match those kids with a couple so they would have mentors of both genders.

Once the mentors start meeting regularly with their kids, what type of contact do you have with them?

We check in with them every month. Either by phone or e-mail, we check in to see how the relationship is going, and what we can do to support them. Our goal is to figure out if there's anything more they need from us.

DEEP MINISTRY

One benefit of checking in that has surprised us is that we can give an outside perspective that's often encouraging to the mentor. When mentors are in the trenches doing the work, often they miss little steps of progress. But when we check in with them and hear how their kids are doing, we can give them reminders of ways their kids are improving compared to what they shared with us the previous month.

After that initial six hours, do you offer any additional training?

You bet. We do quarterly training with our mentors. Usually we invite professionals from the community to come and talk to our mentors about some of the issues we hear them asking about. Those topics have included relationship-building skills, supporting the student's family, substance abuse, and how to relate effectively with the school system. Our list of training topics is constantly changing based on the needs of our mentors.

Asking adults for one to two hours a week is no small request. Do you ever have adults who say they can't make that type of commitment but still want to be involved?

All the time. When that happens, we ask those adults to visit kids in shelters or detention facilities periodically. Sometimes those end up growing into weekly relationships. Simply hanging out with kids is a great starting point for people who want to test the waters before going deeper.

DEEP DESIGN PROMPT

STEP 1: NOW? STEP 3: WHO?

STEP 4: HOW? STEP 2: NEW?

In the midst of all you've learned about mentoring, what are you still trying to figure out?

How to get more people involved. Almost every mentor who gets involved with S.O.Y. ends up saying something like, "Wow, I can't believe how blessed I am. I thought I was doing this to bless someone else, but my life is now transformed." I wish I could figure out how to take that experience and plant it in every adult so they all would decide to make a difference in kids' lives.

DEEP DESIGN, STEP 4 (APPLICATION): *HOW?*

Application Questions:

1. What is your definition of mentoring? If we were to ask others in your ministry for their definitions, what would they say? How do these compare and contrast with the definition of mentoring as "empowering others toward God's purposes for their lives"?

2. This chapter identified three myths about mentoring: something is better than nothing; once you recruit your mentors, your work is done; and you can become the end-all, be-all mentor. Which of these myths is most common in your ministry?

3. After reading this chapter, how would you describe the training you give your mentors?

4. If you were to view mentoring along a continuum of intensity, how would that affect you, your mentors, and your students?

5. How is your situation similar to S.O.Y.? How is it different?

6. Given your reading and reflection, how can you take your mentoring ministry to a deeper level?

How are we going to go deeper in our mentoring?	Source

CHAPTER 7

DEEP PARENTS: "OFF MY BACK" OR "ON THE TEAM"?

Chap Clark

DEEP DESIGN, STEP 1 (DISCERNMENT): *NOW?*

The Story of Mytown Community Church (a fictitious church that could be somewhere near you)

The members of Mytown Community Church have always prided themselves in "caring about our youth." Parents are active and vocal in constantly pushing the church to get its act together and maintain a "solid" youth ministry program. The church, however, had never before had the luxury of a full-time youth director. So when Josh arrived, everyone was excited. Finally, they had a youth director with a youth ministry degree from a Christian college. He was everything they'd hoped for—mid-20s, good speaker, funny, "cool," and passionate.

Josh used his charisma to develop a fairly high-energy program with events that most kids enjoyed. Soon after arriving Josh moved his office next to the youth room, which allowed him to come and go as he pleased through the seldom-used side door of the church office building. He recruited a handful of volunteers to "help him do his ministry," but made sure he was in charge of the "important things"—speaking, vision-casting, decision-making, and handling money. After several months on the job, Josh felt as though he had developed a pretty successful and fruitful ministry.

But the honeymoon began to fade—and fade fast—sometime early in Josh's second year. He heard murmurs that a few parents were "concerned" about some of his decisions. He was so busy being with kids and planning the programs, however, that he figured his successes would cancel out any problems people may have with him. As the months went on, Josh developed an independent and (to some) somewhat "stealth" style of doing his job—spending lots of time with students and a few leaders but avoiding anyone who might "become a problem." Unfortunately, to Josh, that meant parents.

It didn't take long for a few of the more vocal parents to start a movement to ask questions about some "weak spots" in the youth ministry program. These parents felt they were protecting the kids of the church. Josh saw it differently. He felt the ringleaders were out to get him. So he simply kept his head down, avoided the "troublemakers," and did the best job he could—hoping the parents would ease up eventually.

They didn't.

Some parents decided to meet to discuss the "youth ministry situation." They expressed concern that Josh was giving more attention to local athletes and neighborhood students than to the church kids. These conversations began to pick up steam, and soon rumors were flying that Josh was a "lone ranger" who "does his own thing" and "isn't accountable to anyone." As the gossip intensified, Josh circled the wagons with his closest supporters and virtually ignored everyone else in the church. The latest tiff was sparked by the accusation that he wasn't returning phone calls, and when he did respond, it was by e-mail, avoiding any direct conversation.

When the senior pastor finally talked to him, Josh said responding to calls by e-mail was "more efficient" in light of all he had to do. In his exchange with the senior pastor, who had done his best to support him, Josh became more negative about church parents who "don't get it" when it comes to kids or youth ministry. Josh wanted his boss to back him up because, after all, he was the adolescent expert in the church. The pastor recognized that many students were growing in their walks with Christ, and most parents felt good about the ministry. But the voices of concern were loud enough that he had to do something.

Seeing a major storm building on the horizon, Josh's pastor arranged for a face-to-face meeting between Josh and the parents.

The meeting was a disaster. From the beginning it was obvious that feelings ran deep for many of the parents, and they wanted to make sure they were heard. Feeling misunderstood and unfairly accused, Josh came into the meeting ready to defend his education, training, and track record. In less than 10 minutes Josh and the parents became polarized, with one parent finally storming out of the room, loudly vowing to "get that kid fired." It never got better, and Josh was gone by his second June.

Reflection on Mytown Community Church

In my years of youth ministry leadership, I've heard the story of Mytown Community Church countless times. I once received a paper from a student that was entitled "How to Get Parents off Your Back and on Your Team." The entire project (which didn't receive a stellar grade) reflected a view of parents and youth ministry similar to Josh's at Mytown Community. Parents were described as a "necessary nuisance" youth workers have to deal with in order to survive. The paper intended to describe a strategy for vocational youth workers that would entice and keep parents in line with the youth ministry's plans, goals, and structure. But the project was simply a more creative and proactive response to the same attitude prevailing at Mytown Community.

The **Now** of youth ministry and parents assumes that youth ministry belongs to youth workers, and parents just need to get with the program. Parents can be a pain, the thinking goes, so what's the best way to handle them?

But this fundamentally flawed perspective can undo even the best youth ministry programs. When committed

parents feel disconnected from the spiritual development of their 11- to 18-year-olds, they get nervous. If they *feel* like they're being ignored or placated by those in charge of youth ministry, they may respond with destructive behavior. The issue comes down to how parents feel when they are shut out of their child's spiritual journey. Let's take a quick look at just three of the many ways this kind of attitude toward parents can impede even the best youth programs.

DEEP DESIGN PROMPT

Hindering God's transformation: Our attitude toward parents can make or break a youth ministry program over the long haul.

1. When parents are seen as people to placate—or even manipulate if necessary—in order to do the work youth ministry is "supposed" to do, this will inevitably create distance between parents and youth workers. Parents will become everything from complacent and uninvolved to frustrated and resentful. In the long run none of these options helps foster deep youth ministry.

2. When we see parents as potential problems to be strategically handled, we cannot help but feel like we must take over the discipleship role.

3. When we believe parents don't really belong anywhere near the center of our ministries, and we have to placate them into joining "our" team, we will invariably communicate to students that their parents don't really matter all that much. Unfortunately, we know the opposite is true about the hearts and needs of kids—their parents matter, and ultimately they matter a whole lot more than youth workers. Many parents already feel the tension and heartache of losing touch with their kids, especially during high school. When we communicate, even subtly, that parents don't matter (using phrases like, "they don't get it," "they don't understand you," or "they are out of touch"), we deepen the divide that neither par-

DEEP DESIGN PROMPT

Hindering God's transformation: If we treat parents as outsiders, or problems, or unimportant, that ultimately hurts students.

ents nor adolescents really want. Instead of being an advocate for family healing and wholeness, we can easily end up doing damage and bringing more strife to already fragile and tenuous relationships.

WHEN PARENTS ARE SEEN AS A NUISANCE …

- Parents are treated as a roadblock, causing distance between the youth worker and parents.
- We place ourselves as the central discipleship figure for students instead of the parent(s) and the church.
- We communicate to students that their parents don't matter much anymore.

7.1

In far too many churches and parachurch organizations, parents are **Now** seen as necessary supporters to the youth ministry, but also as people who get in the way all too often. Sooner or later parents will begin to resent this attitude, and cracks will form in the church. Could there be a *deeper* way to view the relationships between parents and youth workers?

∞ DEEP DESIGN PROMPT

STEP 1: NOW?   STEP 3: WHO?

STEP 4: HOW?   **STEP 2: NEW?**

DEEP DESIGN, STEP 2 (REFLECTION): *NEW?*

When it comes to the relationship between youth workers and parents, the fundamental question we must ask is *what do developing adolescents need in terms of adult nurture and guidance?* Although it's clear that peers play an important role in the developmental life of teenagers, research has shown that a network of adult relational support, committed to the long-term care and growth of adolescents, plays a profound role in providing the kind of relational support they need to grow into the people God created them to be.[35] This network, however, is clearly

[35] See William Damon, *The Youth Charter*, New York: Free Press, 1997.

DEEP MINISTRY

secondary to the impact of a child's family, in both positive and negative ways.[36]

What adolescents need, then, is the *intersection* and *partnership* of parents (or at least one parent or caretaker) available and focused on them as individuals, and adults representing the church and committed to their spiritual and life development.[37] Research has shown that youth workers can play a part—sometimes a vital part—in the spiritual development of teenagers. But parents play a much greater role over the long haul for the vast majority of kids.[38] To provide the best possible environment for spiritual growth to take place in adolescents' lives, parents and youth workers need each other.

Social science research points to the need for a focused partnership between parents and youth ministry, but what does the Bible say? Or, to put it another way, how is God asking youth workers to respond to and work with parents?

Depending on what Scripture passage you look up, or even whom you read or listen to, you can easily come away from the Bible being fully convinced in one direction or another about parents' places in youth ministry—they are either esteemed as partners or strategized as potential obstacles. And when these two polar-opposite viewpoints ignore or deny each other, they become deep ditches that cause us to fall off the path God laid out for us. Let's look more carefully at these two extremes, or ditches, of parents and youth ministry.

> ∞ **DEEP DESIGN PROMPT**
> Research: Parents and other committed adults in partnership are adolescents' best chance at healthy growth.

> ∞ **DEEP DESIGN PROMPT**
> Scripture: The Bible seems to both support and discourage parents' involvement in the spiritual development of their kids. How do we decide what to do?

DITCH 1: Jesus, my friends, and me

The ditch on one side of the road is the dangerous belief that parents don't matter—all that matters to God is our love for him and our commitment to his body, the church (meaning for most teenagers, the youth ministry). Jesus himself is the one who seems to say parents don't matter

---

[36] See David Elkind, *Ties That Stress*, Cambridge, MA: Harvard University Press, 1994, and David Elkind, *The Hurried Child* (3rd ed.) Cambridge, MA: Perseus, 2001.

[37] Jeffrey J. Arnett, *Adolescence and Emerging Adulthood*, Upper Saddle River, NJ: Pearson Education, 2000.

[38] See Chap Clark, *Hurt* (Grand Rapids, MI: Baker Academic, 2005).

in one's spiritual life. Take this statement, when Jesus was told his mom and brothers were outside of the house:

> He replied to him, "Who is my mother, and who are my brothers?" Pointing to his disciples, he said, "Here are my mother and my brothers. For whoever does the will of my Father in heaven is my brother and sister and mother." (Matthew 12:48-50)

In Luke's Gospel, Jesus' words are even more pointed:

> Then, responding to the large crowds who were following him, Jesus said, "If anyone comes to me and does not hate his father and mother, his wife and children, his brothers and sisters—yes, even his own life—he cannot be my disciple." (Luke 14:25-26)

On the basis of a few selected passages like these, some in youth ministry have developed a kind of "all that matters is my love for Jesus" mentality that almost always translates into a ministry style that communicates faith as individualistic and only to be experienced with those I naturally trust. For adolescents, this means a handful of leaders and friends, with parents and other adults taking a marginal role at best. This "me and Jesus" attitude excludes parents in a way God never intended. Jesus' point is that our call to be his disciples must be so central to who we are and how we live that no one else will get in the way of that commitment. By taking certain statements alone—out of context from the rest of Scripture—some people have mistakenly assumed that God doesn't really care about how other people contribute to our lives as disciples. When this view is emphasized to the point where student disciples think they *only* need Jesus and a few friends, God's plan for the body of Christ

and life together in community is ignored and our program and attitude lands us in a ditch.

DITCH 2: My family is my church

The ditch on the other side of the road is one where parents are seen as the "primary disciplers" of their children, even through adolescence. Although this perspective has lost some steam in recent years, it still has quite a hold in many traditions and churches, and is sometimes defended by family ministry advocates. As the movement toward family ministry became more central in youth ministry discussions,[39] and as the homeschooling movement became more mainstream, many saw youth ministry as taking kids *away* from their families. Those reacting to the abuses of youth ministries' independence, especially as it related to parents' authority and leadership in kids' lives, used Scriptures such as these to prove their point:

> "These are the commands, decrees and laws the Lord your God directed me to teach you to observe in the land that you are crossing the Jordan to possess, so that you, your children and their children after them may fear the Lord your God as long as you live…
>
> "Hear, O Israel: The Lord our God, the Lord is one. Love the Lord your God with all your heart and with all your soul and with all your strength. These commandments that I give you today are to be upon your hearts. Impress them on your children. Talk about them when you sit at home and when you walk along the road, when you lie down and when you get up. Tie them as symbols on your hands and bind them on your foreheads. Write them on the doorframes of your houses and on your gates." (Deuteronomy 6:1-9)[40]

[39] Beginning with Mark DeVries' book, *Family-Based Youth Ministry* (Downer's Grove, IL: IVP, 1994), there was a flood of articles, lectures, and books seeking to increase the involvement of parents and families in youth ministry, urging ministers to view parents as partners. While the majority of youth workers would probably say this is their understanding, the fact is that most youth workers and programs fall into one of these two ditches.

[40] Although we won't go into it here, there is ample evidence that this passage is meant for the adult community at large rather than just a mom and dad.

"Children, obey your parents in the Lord, for this is right." (Ephesians 6:1)

"Children, obey your parents in everything, for this pleases the Lord." (Colossians 3:20)[41]

∞ DEEP DESIGN PROMPT

History: Some parents have used the Bible to debunk their kids' need for peer and nonparental adult influence in their spiritual development.

When these verses are used to diminish the role of youth ministry in kids' lives, the common explanation is that whenever the Bible talks about children, parents are the ones who are responsible to lead them. In this ditch, parents' roles in the discipleship of their children become *overemphasized* to the point where other adults, including paid and volunteer youth workers, are seen as potential obstacles to healthy growth in Christ. This interpretation of selected passages seems to ignore the necessary role other people play in all levels of spiritual development and discipleship.[42] The Bible makes it clear that we need one another to function as God intends.[43] When a philosophy of raising children (and adolescents) ignores the need for a greater community beyond the nuclear family during the discipling process, youth lose out on God's plan for their development. This ditch hurts kids because God never intended any of us to go it alone in raising our children.

The Middle Path: Youth Workers and Parents Need Each Other to Minister to Students

While the Bible passages the two camps quote may seem contradictory at first, upon further careful reflection they are shown to be complementary. Jesus repeatedly warned that life is found only when we center our lives on him.[44] But he also said the one command he has for us is to "love one another" (John 15:12). To love Jesus first does not contradict the biblical truth that we need one another.

---

[41] Ephesians 5:22-6:9 and Colossians 3:18-22 are considered examples of the apostle Paul's "household rules," a common way writers and leaders of his day taught people how to live orderly lives.

[42] Regarding the Deuteronomy passage, many scholars suggest the phrase "Impress them on your children" is directed just as much to the whole community as it is to the nuclear family.

[43] See 1 Corinthians 12 and Romans 12 for examples of the different gifts we all need to experience from and with one another.

[44] John 15:1-8.

The irony is that both ditches share the same fatal flaw: each group has decided it is the essential element that will lead adolescents to Jesus Christ. Those in the "all kids need is Jesus" ditch see the youth worker as the primary broker of kids' relationship with Christ, often at the expense of parental nurture. On the other hand, those in the "our family can handle it" ditch view the rest of the church, including youth workers, as a hindrance to their work with their kids. In reality, the Bible affirms that parents need other adults (and therefore youth workers), and the church (in the person of the youth workers) needs parents—and kids need both. Children and adolescents need their parents to protect, nurture, and guide them in all areas of their lives, including their spiritual growth; but at the same time, God's people throughout history have expressed their faith as a *community* where there is a common bond and a shared story. This community, in fact, is actually called "family" in the new covenant Jesus came to bring—we are God's family, and we belong to and need each other.[45]

Looking *theologically* at the issue of parents in youth ministry, it seems there's no doubt that we're called to *walk between these ditches*. It is true, both in the Bible and in what we know about development, that parents are key players in the lives of children. And it is also true that the vast majority of students will experience a more lasting impact from parental involvement in their spiritual lives than from anything youth ministry can offer.[46] When the body of Christ (the church and those who represent it—youth workers) and parents of adolescents work together, students have the best opportunity at discovering the Christ-centered community as the place where they will always be welcome in an often cold and hostile world.

∞ DEEP DESIGN PROMPT

Research: Kids need both their parents and the greater body of Christ—including peers and youth ministry workers—to grow as disciples.

---

[45] See Galatians 6:10 and Ephesians 3:15.
[46] For the most up-to-date research on adolescent religious attitudes, see National Study of Youth and Religion (http://www.youthandreligion.org, accessed September 3, 2005) and Christian Smith and Melinda L. Denton, ibid.

Your ability to work well with parents depends first on your attitude toward them. Parents can *sense* how much you value their input and involvement in the ministry and whether or not you're sincere in the way you deal with them. You may believe, for example, that you have a pretty solid perspective of the value of parents, but if you don't make sure parental involvement permeates every aspect of your ministry and program, parents will start to distrust you. When you announce a new midweek afternoon Bible study for middle school students at the church, but don't think through the transportation needs for kids of working parents, some parents will be deeply affected, and even hurt. Even those who aren't inconvenienced by this decision could see you as a youth worker who doesn't care about the needs and realities of today's families.

To have a *deep ministry* with parents, we must do more than work on our surface attitudes and resulting programming and structure. We also must be aware of other external factors that can cause a problem with parents, even when our attitudes and programming are on target. Three of these factors are your own life stage, the history of your church, and the way you organize your ministry.

 **DEEP DESIGN PROMPT**

Experience: Most parents don't believe that youth workers who've never raised adolescent children have much to say to parents about parenting.

Your Life Stage

The simple fact is that the average youth worker has never been through the labyrinth of raising a child through adolescence. As much as it might bug us to admit it, we need to be honest about this: there really is no way we can *truly* understand what it means and how it feels to be a parent if we've never been one. Trying to deny this or convince parents that you know more about kids (and remember: to parents, theirs are the only kids who matter) will drive a wedge between you and them that could be insurmountable. So if this is you, swallow hard, and come in as a

humble and respectful support, not a hero who knows students better than their parents.

The History of Your Church or Organization

History affects us—even if we had nothing to do with the events of the past. We have to account for this fact as we attempt to make a difference. A few years ago my friend Brook bought a coffee shop that had caused a major fire in a strip mall. For the next three years, the other tenants in the mall blamed Brook for the fire, even though they knew logically that he'd not been involved. His only recourse was to slowly yet proactively build bridges of trust, allowing people to see he was different from the previous owner.

If you're in a church or organization that has created some bad blood with parents in the past, follow Brook's lead—don't try to defend yourself before people know you. Come alongside parents, communicate well with them, and structure a ministry that includes them as partners. When problems arise—and they will—and people start bringing up the past, make sure you stay the course of love and inclusion. Over time, being different will win over even the people who were most burned in the past.

> ∞ **DEEP DESIGN PROMPT**
>
> Experience: Regardless of how strained the parent-youth worker relationship was in the past, you can overcome that history by taking time to build bridges and win trust.

The Organization of Your Ministry

When you begin a new ministry (or revamp a current one), the first thing to do is to create a group of people (mostly parents) to walk with you as you implement your ministry. Several youth workers are now using an idea called the Vision and Support Team (VAST) to fulfill this need.[47] (We'll look at VAST more in the **Who** section of this chapter.)

VAST is much more than a parents council. All too often a parents council ends up being little more than a

---

[47] The VAST idea is included in Chap Clark, *Youth Worker's Handbook to Family Ministry*, Grand Rapids: Zondervan, 1997. See also Marv Penner, *Youth Worker's Guide to Parent Ministry*, Grand Rapids: Zondervan, 2003 and Jim Burns and Mike Devries, *Partnering with Parents in Youth Ministry*, Ventura, CA: Regal, 2003 for lots of ideas on partnering with parents.

∞ **DEEP DESIGN PROMPT**

Experience: Create an adult team, including some parents, to partner with you in developing vision and providing insight and support for the youth ministry.

rubber-stamp group that's called upon to support blindly whatever the youth leader wants. To be on the Vision and Support Team, people have to demonstrate a commitment to *all* students the ministry is called to reach (including those who don't currently call the church home). While parents are strongly encouraged to serve on the team, they would participate not as a "parent of one," but would be encouraged to share in the visioning as well as the implementation of that vision.

In addition to a leadership body that includes parents and functions as a partnering and accountability board, the most important way to organize your ministry around a commitment to partnering with parents is to ask them to help you. Build friendships with parents. Invite criticism and feedback. Do a yearly survey of parents *and follow up with a report of the results.* Send notes and letters regularly to keep the lines of communication open. In general, make sure that the way you go about your work reminds parents that they are vital partners in the student ministry.

∞ **DEEP DESIGN PROMPT**

STEP 1: NOW?   **STEP 3: WHO?**

STEP 4: HOW?   STEP 2: NEW?

DEEP DESIGN, STEP 3 (OBSERVATION): *WHO?*

Instead of highlighting a specific youth worker or program, we've decided to pull together the best practices of several churches and programs in one composite youth ministry. Like the fictional *Mytown Community Church* that opens this chapter, *First United Church* exists in a variety of places and expressions, so we felt that putting it all together in one illustration would help you find a way to include the **New** insight in your program.

The Story of First United Church

When the new youth director arrived at United, the students were excited, but frankly, most of the parents were

relatively neutral about him. Rob had never been a head youth minister before—he'd always worked as an associate youth pastor under someone else. But he was honest and open about his strengths and weaknesses. Although he was not a great speaker, the students who had spent time with him felt as though he genuinely understood them and cared. He was up front about his lack of organizational skills and the fact that he was at his best on a team, so he insisted on bringing one of his former interns, Katie, to codirect and partner with him.

The first thing Rob and Katie did was form a Vision and Support Team (VAST), a group of parents and other adults who weren't involved as leaders but were nevertheless invested in kids' lives. Rob and Katie's desire was to design a ministry structure in which non-leader adults and parents were integrally involved in the major decision-making and strategic vision process of the ministry. Rob and Katie spent the bulk of their first year trying to get to know students within the context of their families, since they believed youth ministry means partnering with the parents and the church at large in reaching out to students. This included a student ministry letter sent to families every month, quarterly parent meetings, and parenting seminars (with the children's and adult education departments) every six months.

During the second year, a group of parents became upset that their children were not responding to the youth programs and were starting to go to another church with a flashier ministry. VAST and Rob and Katie arranged a meeting with those who had expressed concern and invited the senior pastor and board chair to come. Rob and the head of VAST cochaired the meeting, opening with a reading from the Psalms and a brief time of prayer. The VAST chair then invited the concerned (and to some extent, disgruntled) parents to express their feelings and opinions, while Rob and Katie took notes. When the parents had finished, Rob and Katie thanked them for sharing their concerns and then restated them to be sure they'd heard the issues correctly. After that, the meeting moved into a free-flowing discussion about how to respond to the issues at hand. The parents left without a clean or clear solution, but with a sense of hope that the church supported them and cared about their concerns. They ended the meeting in prayer.

Rob is currently in his tenth year and is now the pastor of youth and families. Katie, a mom herself, is the high school director. The ministry is flourishing, parents are involved at all levels, and kids feel as though they are known and loved by the congregation as a whole. Although Rob is still an average speaker at best and remains somewhat disorganized, the church would do anything to make sure he and his family knows they're valued and loved.

In the two churches we've looked at (which are composites of actual churches and youth workers I've known over the last few years), one youth worker (Josh) found himself in hot water because of his cavalier and dismissive attitudes and behavior toward parents (especially "concerned" parents!). Katie and Rob, on the other hand, began their ministry by proactively and strategically including parents at every level. When problems arose, as they will for any youth pastor, they not only had built the infrastructure for the best possible setting to deal with conflict, but they also dealt with conflict directly, adult to adult. A savvy youth worker, I suppose, could apply the *strategy* that Rob and Katie used—forming a Vision and Support Team, generating regular newsletters, organizing meetings and events for parents, and providing a welcoming atmosphere to air problems—without a heart that believes parents matter. But from my experience, this isn't something you can fake. Either you believe that parents are partners, or you don't.

DEEP DESIGN, STEP 4 (APPLICATION): *HOW?*

∞ DEEP DESIGN PROMPT

STEP 1: NOW?   STEP 3: WHO?

STEP 4: HOW?   STEP 2: NEW?

Application Questions:

1. This chapter discussed youth workers at two churches with opposing perspectives regarding parents and youth ministry—Josh, the youth worker who saw parents as a secondary concern at best, versus Rob and Katie, who built their program around parents as partners. In what ways do you tend to act more like Josh, and in what ways are you more like Katie and Rob?

2. When you consider the Bible passages included here (and others), where do you stand on the relationship of youth ministry to parents?

3. What has been your experience working with parents? Have you had any conflicts with parents in your ministry? If so, do you feel as though you navigated them well? If the conflicts didn't end well, how could you have handled them differently?

4. What are three ways you can go deep in taking parents more seriously as partners?

How are we going to go deeper in our partnering with parents?	Source

SECTION 3
DEEPER PRACTICES

CHAPTER 8

DEEP COMMUNICATION: WHY DOESN'T OUR TEACHING CHANGE KIDS' LIVES?

Chap Clark

∞ **DEEP DESIGN PROMPT**

Hindering God's transformation: Our main goal for communication often becomes entertaining kids.

DEEP DESIGN, STEP 1 (DISCERNMENT): *NOW?*

Jim Rayburn, the founder of Young Life, is famous for saying, "It's a sin to bore a kid." When it comes to our teaching, most youth workers hear that and feel as though we have a lot of confessing to do! Even for those youth workers who are usually able to keep kids laughing, interested, and glued to the edge of their chairs (in some cases, literally), a statement like that can become little more than a guilt-producing incentive to keep them "liking" what we do.

Many of us hope that during our merry-go-rounds of programming, kids are interested in and excited by the worship (usually a fancy word for singing), willing to laugh and be (more or less) quiet during our "talks," and willing to be semi-committed and quasi-vulnerable in small groups. To an awful lot of us, this *is* youth ministry. When pressed, most of us probably hope that in the midst of that programmatic machine our kids will develop an internal desire to learn about God—and thus pursue him eventually on their own.

If we are honest, however, somewhere deep inside we know it's our job as youth workers to prompt and prod our students into considering the complex texture and depth of the gospel. We know that teaching matters—Jesus himself said so ("…teaching them to obey all that I have commanded you…" Matthew 28:20; see Chapter 4 for more on this). But when we spend our precious few minutes of teaching trying to be relevant and funny, showing cool movie clips, we end up with so little time to delve into the Bible with any depth that we, at some level, fail our students.

Some youth workers have addressed this by relegating Bible study to small groups. But in many of those situations, the environment seems to encourage "sharing" around the Word rather than seriously diving into

the Scriptures. Somehow we need to recapture a deep approach to speaking and teaching that involves a thorough study of the text as well as a hunger for the things of God as revealed in his Word.

DEEP DESIGN, STEP 2 (REFLECTION): *NEW?*

In studying the religious attitudes and behaviors of adolescents, human development researchers Jeffrey J. Arnett and Lene A. Jensen report the following four characteristics:

∞ **DEEP DESIGN PROMPT**

STEP 1: NOW?   STEP 3: WHO?

STEP 4: HOW?   **STEP 2: NEW?**

- Their beliefs are highly individualized

- They are skeptical of religious institutions

- Denominational affiliation means little, and

- Childhood socialization toward religion has limited effects.

Essentially, they found that because adolescents "view it as both their right and their responsibility to form their beliefs and values independently from their parents, they pick and choose from the ideas they discover as they go along, and combine them to form their own unique, individualized set of beliefs, an *'a la carte* belief system.'" They concluded that, although religion is centrally important for adolescents, it is also highly relative and private— "in a congregation of one."[48]

∞ **DEEP DESIGN PROMPT**

Research: Students' faith is highly relative and private, "in a congregation of one."

This conclusion has been confirmed in several studies since, most notably in the extensive study conducted by the National Study of Youth and Religion (NSYR), led by Christian Smith, principal researcher and professor of sociology at University of North Carolina, Chapel Hill.[49] Given kids' attitudes toward faith, it is our job not only to win hearts but also to captivate the minds of today's adolescents who are "individualized, skeptical of religious

[48] Arnett, J. J. & Jensen, L. A. (2002). "A Congregation of One: Individualized religious beliefs among emerging adults," (pp. 84-94). In Jeffrey J. Arnett, *Readings on Adolescence and Emerging Adulthood*. Upper Saddle River, NJ: Prentice Hall, 93. At publication, this article can be accessed at http://jar.sagepub.com/cgi/content/abstract/17/5/451.

[49] See Christian Smith and M. L. Denton, *Soul Searching: The Religious and Spiritual Lives of America's Teenagers* (Oxford: Oxford University Press, 2005).

institutions," and who lack loyalty toward their parents' denominations and traditions.

∞ DEEP DESIGN PROMPT

Experience: Kids may not look as though they want to wrestle with new and challenging information, but they DO!

But there is hope, and lots of it, when we set out to engage young disciples' minds. Many youth ministry leaders, including Kara and me, affirm that today's kids are *eager* to learn and be stretched in their understanding of God. Our problem is figuring out the best way to turn that key and get them motivated to go deeper in their faith. This chapter offers three vital principles to help youth workers become more effective and solid communicators as they seek to engage the minds of students.

KEEP THESE PRINCIPLES IN MIND WHEN COMMUNICATING TO STUDENTS

#1 – Communication is the art of being understood.

#2 – Persuasion is more complicated than it seems.

#3 – God is the one who transforms.

8.1

Principle 1: Recognize That Communication Is the Art of Being Understood[50]

Most of us have grown up believing communication is only about delivery. As long as I've said, or taught, or written something, I have communicated. But communication studies scholars recognized long ago that communication is not complete until someone has *received* the message being sent.

∞ DEEP DESIGN PROMPT

Research: We can't communicate if we don't understand the kids we're communicating to.

Because communication requires that we do all we can to ensure that students understand what we're trying to

---

[50] This phrase is so common that the original source is impossible to determine.

[51] S. Harter, S. Bresnick, H. A. Boushey, & N. R. Whitesell, J. J. Arnett, & L. A. Jensen (2002). The Complexity of the Self in Adolescence. (111-119). In Jeffrey J. Arnett, *Readings on Adolescence and Emerging Adulthood*, Upper Saddle River, NJ: Prentice Hall, 112. The authors state, "During adolescence, it has been shown that adolescents develop a proliferation of selves that vary as a function of the social context. These include self with father, mother, close friend, romantic partner, peers, as well as the self in the role of student, on the job, and as athlete … A critical developmental task of adolescence, therefore, is the construction of multiple selves in different roles and relationships."

pass on to them, we have to keep in mind who our kids are whenever we try to communicate with them. This is true no matter what form or medium we use—talks, songs, written words, and even images.

In terms of teaching and speaking, there are three facts about adolescents that can help us communicate and connect with them more clearly. First, we need to remember that as their identities are being formed during adolescence, most young people live out of "multiple selves."[51] Kids will have one "self" they live out of at school (actually several, because in each class and activity they need to live out of the "self" that's safest for them at the time), another "self" at home, and still another "self" at your ministry.[52] They also feel the need to express these selves differently in the various roles they assume in their lives—such as with sports, in different classes, at church, and at home. This in turn causes them to stay on guard constantly to determine which role is the most appropriate to "put on" in any given setting.[53]

Knowing that all students are obsessed with their social environments and the roles they play within them can help us realize that much of what we receive in feedback (or lack of feedback) may not be about our message (or us) at all. But it also means we may have some work to do to get them focused on the issues at hand. We will work on **How** in a few pages, but for now, understanding the mindsets of your students will go a long way toward your connecting with them.

∞ DEEP DESIGN PROMPT

Research: Students have "multiple selves" and are preoccupied with what others think of them.

Second, and related, is the fact that adolescents are intensely aware of the possibility of having their feelings hurt and guard against this constantly.[54] Even though you may not be able to see it directly, adolescents are intuitively aware of how fragile they are, and often believe they are one social miscue from being cast aside by friends. A stray

---

[52] See Chap Clark, *Hurt: Inside the World of Today's Teenagers,* Grand Rapids, MI: Baker Academic, 2005, for a detailed discussion and analysis of living out of the multiple selves.

[53] This is referred to as "layered living." See Clark, *Hurt.*

[54] Anita L. Vangelisti, Stacy L. Young, Katy E. Carpenter-Theune, and Alicia L. Alexander, "Why Does It Hurt?: The Perceived Causes of Hurt Feelings," *Communication Research,* Vol. 32, No. 4, 443-477 (2005).

DEEP DESIGN PROMPT

Research: Students are easily hurt.

word, a sideways glance, or an inappropriate illustration or phrase can send one or more youth group members over the emotional edge. Whenever we take the floor to deliver a message—and it can be anything from an announcement to a prayer—we hold great power. Students know this, and they're also aware of how this power can turn around and hurt them at any moment. It's not that we would intend to cause pain, but regardless of our intent, the impact hurts. To connect with them in meaningful ways, we have to overcome their instinctual fear of potential harm (*and* be really, really careful).

Third, any time adolescents believe they are in a potentially hostile environment (which is almost everywhere they go, even youth ministry settings), they are expecting at some level to be evaluated and criticized. Studies have consistently shown that all of us are more open to processing messages if we believe they'll help us develop better moods.[55] Many students in our programs will assume our messages will be boring at best and guilt-producing downers at worst. If we *start* with them thinking we are out to get them, or that the message we offer will give them no sense of hope, they'll do all they can to avoid listening to us. When we offer words of encouragement and hope, our message has a better chance of taking root.

DEEP DESIGN PROMPT

Research: Students are looking for positive, encouraging messages.

COMMUNICATION: THE ART OF BEING UNDERSTOOD UNDERSTANDING YOUR STUDENTS

Adolescents live out of "multiple selves."

Adolescents are wary of getting hurt or made fun of.

Adolescents are looking for positive and encouraging messages.

8.2

---

[55] Craig R. Hullett "The Impact of Mood on Persuasion: A Meta-Analysis," *Communication Research*, Vol. 32, No. 4, 423-442 (2005). See also Clark, *Hurt*.

There's no doubt that adolescents are desperate for safe environments.[56] They want places where they can let down their guards. They want to be able to trust that those in charge are going to make sure that the church (or any Christian setting) is one place where they don't have to work so hard at the role(s) they play. They also need to know that the message we offer them is the most encouraging, hope-filled, and refreshingly uplifting message they could ever hope to receive. This is the beginning of communication—making sure our students expect and look forward to the beauty and healing majesty of the gospel message.

Principle 2: Persuasion Is More Complicated Than It Seems

In youth ministry, we partner with the Holy Spirit's work in kids' lives by loving them as God loves them. We seek to *persuade* students, without an agenda demanding a response, to consider who God is and what his call is for their lives. With students, then, our ultimate goal is to somehow convince them to *change*—change their minds, change their lifestyles, change their habits, and sometimes even change how they choose their friends and activities. The apostle Paul said, "We try to persuade people" (2 Corinthians 5:11, TNIV), and so do we in youth ministry. In fact, that's our job! We want kids to be so convinced by the gospel that they hand their lives over to the Holy Spirit, who is the one who does the changing.

DEEP DESIGN PROMPT

Scripture: We, like Paul, are called to persuade.

Every time we're confronted with messages seeking to persuade us, we have to make a series of choices. Look at the Communication Decision Steps diagram. First, we have to decide whether we'll allow this person or message to get through to us (in youth ministry we've seen *that* one up close!). Then, we need to decide how much we'll let our own opinions and feelings influence what's being asked of us. Finally, we must decide to what degree we'll

DEEP DESIGN PROMPT

Research: In the communication process, students face three points of decision.

---

[56] See Elkind, *The Hurried Child*, and Clark, *Hurt*.

allow the message to confront our carefully crafted perspectives and whether we're willing to change our minds about whatever the message is saying. So our task is to help our students say "yes" at all three points in this decision process.

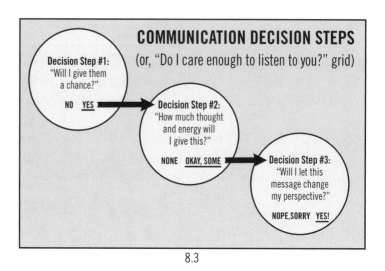

8.3

In any type of communication, whether speaking or teaching or counseling, we must do all we can to persuade without causing our receivers to tune us out or become defensive (see "6 Behaviors That Promote Defensiveness"). To do this we must work to get beyond the walls and defense mechanisms teenagers are so good at using. Sometimes our teaching falls flat because we haven't done the work of building relationships with our students—or because it's Sunday morning, and they are exhausted. But often the problem is that we haven't considered how they think or feel about a given issue or topic. We generally have little idea what their internal, deeply held initial attitudes are coming into a lesson or message.

As someone who's been doing this a long time, I've noticed that it's much harder to "win the right to be heard" with kids today than it was in the 1970s. But at the same time, once youth do show interest, they're often far more engaged than students 30 years ago. So, grabbing their attention may be a bit tougher now, but once they are there, great things can happen. Add to this the nature of the gospel's call—to share "with gentleness and respect"[57] as opposed to trying to manipulate or coerce students into the kingdom of God. This is the main difference between self-centered manipulation and loving persuasion—we share the story that has changed us, what we've seen and heard. We are not out to trick anybody into faith; we are fellow travelers with an incredible adventure to hand off.

To help students even begin to engage in the content of the gospel, we need to know what keeps them from caring about what we are trying to communicate. The first step may be as simple as using creative communication techniques instead of just talking at them. We also need to find methods to help students learn in ways that fit their life experiences and how they learn best (what we call *learning styles*).

We will hit techniques, tips, and tools later, but first we must take a hard look at what happens inside the minds of those we're attempting to communicate with (or, if you will, persuade). We'll do this by taking a quick look at *Social Judgment Theory.*[58]

Each person comes to any discussion, small group, class, or program with a fairly sophisticated system of beliefs, attitudes, and values. (This is true of both adults and adolescents.) *Beliefs* are what we think is true; *attitudes* are our predispositions to respond to given situations, and *values* are those things we hold up as important. The more strongly and deeply someone holds onto particular beliefs,

Wondering about the difference between "persuasion" and "manipulation"? Curious about other findings that most youth workers don't know about? Check out www.cyfm.net for a free article that introduces more insights about teaching kids.

DEEP DESIGN PROMPT

Experience: Today's kids are harder to engage, but once they do, they're more willing to go deep.

---

[57] 1 Peter 3:15; see also Colossians 3:12.
[58] See Trenholm, *Persuasion and Social Influence* (New Jersey:Prentice Hall, 1982), for a detailed explanation of Social Judgment Theory.

"Ego-involvement" = the degree to which we're emotionally committed to an issue.

attitudes, and values, the harder it is to disrupt them or challenge them. The goal of Social Judgment Theory is to determine the initial perspective of the person you're trying to reach so you'll have the best shot at inviting them to consider a change.

Social Judgment Theory[59] states that the more people care about something, the more entrenched they will be against differing opinions. For example, let's say you're trying to get a message across to Juan, a high school sophomore with whom you have a great relationship. But he's also let you know that he "has his own opinions." The more "ego-involved" Juan is regarding a particular topic, the harder he will work against persuasion to think differently. Compare Juan with Kerry, who generally doesn't care passionately about most issues (or is not too "ego involved") and is somewhat neutral to persuasive appeals unless something causes her to sit up and take notice. If both Juan and Kerry become convinced the issue does matter to them, Kerry will move from apathy to engagement, and Juan will at least give the message a hearing.

---

6 Behaviors That Promote Defensiveness

While no one *causes* our defensiveness, when we sense any of these six behaviors in someone trying to communicate with us, our first reaction is often defensiveness.

- *Superiority*—this person acts as though he/she is better than me

- *Certainty*—if I disagree with this person, he/she will treat me as though I'm stupid and wrong

- *Evaluation of opponents*—this person acts as if he/she knows what I'm thinking

---

[59] C. Sherif, M. Sherif, & R. E. Nebergall, (1965). *Attitude and Attitude Change: The Social Judgment-Involvement Approach.* Philadelphia: Saunders.

> - *Control*—this person is more concerned about leading the discussion than letting it be a give-and-take
>
> - *Neutrality*—what I think doesn't matter to this person
>
> - *Strategy*—this person has a strategy and cares more about that strategy than me

8.4

The logic behind Social Judgment Theory is best described by the Assimilation-Contrast Effect. If someone with high ego-involvement (e.g., Juan, whose initial attitude is entrenched against our position) feels as though a message and appeal is too far from where he is now, he'll probably feel his position is threatened. This will, more than likely, push him even *farther* from your desired change. This is called the *contrast effect*.

But if Juan feels as though your message and appeal respects him and seeks only to get him to move a little toward you, it's more than likely he'll move closer to your position. This is known as the *assimilation effect*. The key is Juan's initial attitude and how open he is to changing his mind.

In youth ministry most of our students resist engaging in our messages either because they don't see a need to care about the topic at hand, or they think what we say may go against what they already feel strongly about.

DEEP DESIGN PROMPT

Research: Sometimes baby steps of persuasion keep threatened people from running the other way.

But how do we persuade people like Kerry who aren't "anti" like Juan but more "neutral," yet still don't want to be persuaded (i.e., the "apathetic church kid syndrome")? Our job as communicators, according to Social Judgment Theory, is to get Kerry "off the fence" and away from a middle, non-ego-involved position. In other words, our task is to get her to *care*, one way or another. After we get her think-

∞ DEEP DESIGN
PROMPT

Research: Social Judg-
ment Theory can help
us to become more
effective communica-
tors to students.

ing about how she feels about the topic, we can begin to help Kerry decide how to respond to our message. When students seem apathetic toward our teaching and talks, we have to help them see a need to engage. Once they realize the issue matters to them, then they can be motivated to move down the road toward growth and change.

> "A *need* is a lack of something an organism considers necessary. A *motive* is an inner state that directs the organism toward the satisfaction of a need."[60]

The following foundational principles can help us be more effective communicators, whether we're talking with Juan or Kerry or anyone in between:

- Each person has an opinion about almost everything.

- Whenever others try to change our minds or alter our opinions, we judge that persuasive appeal according to what we believe already and how deeply we care about it. (Our judgment can also be affected by how much we trust the person making the appeal.)

- The amount of "ego-involvement" will affect how deeply entrenched we are in our positions. (Or, to put it another way, the degree to which we care about something will tell us how far away we think the persuaders are from our position.)

- The more we care about the issues at hand, the quicker and more fiercely we will internally distort and argue against points of view or agendas that challenge our beliefs. (And because our amazing minds can fly at warp speed when threatened, we often write the message off before the persuaders have taken their first breaths.)

[60] Trenholm, *Persuasion and Social Influence*, 239.

- If we believe the difference between our position and another's position is relatively small, in the interest of social harmony we'll tend to drift in the direction of that minor change. (In so doing, our opinion assimilates the position of the person trying to persuade us.)

Implications of Social Judgment Theory for Youth Ministry

What does this have to do with our communication with youth? *Everything*! If we can anticipate and recognize our students' initial attitudes or levels of ego-involvement, we will have a far better chance at getting them to allow their minds to interact with our messages. We have to make sure our speaking or teaching is, first, compelling and interesting enough to warrant them giving our message a chance. Second, we need to make sure our messages line up close enough to their initial attitudes that they aren't threatened by them (but not so close they just flippantly agree with us), while at the same time pushing them a little bit closer to the *end goal* of what we're trying to communicate.

The best way to picture this is on a seven-point scale that measures initial attitudes. Let's say you're talking to students about sexuality. Although you might use different categories, possible initial attitudes may look like this:

CHRISTIAN ADOLESCENT SEXUALITY INITIAL ATTITUDES						
1	2	3	4	5	6	7
All sex okay	All but intercourse okay	All but oral sex okay	Not really sure, but "messing around" is probably okay	Touching and "exploring" okay	Kissing anyone okay	Kissing only in relationship

8.5

Using passages such as Matthew 5:27-28, 1 Thessalonians 4:3-8, and Philippians 4:8, you may want to convince (or *persuade*) your students that God calls us to see intimate sexual behavior as something sacred and therefore expressed only in the context of a loving, committed relationship that the Bible affirms as marriage (not just "love"). If most of your students are between 2 and 4 on the above scale, Social Judgment Theory suggests that the best way to convince them is *not* to try immediately to get them to move to a 7, but rather to get them to think about, discuss, and pray about moving one or two spots to the right. *After* they have moved a little in response to your presentation, your next message should try to persuade them to move a little more (e.g., the next small group meeting can follow up on this teaching). And the next discussion would seek to move them a little more—and so on. In other words, don't try to move them too far all at once, but guide them with respect and gentleness into honest dialogue with the Spirit through the Scriptures.

∞ DEEP DESIGN PROMPT

Scripture: We need to be both bold and gentle.

Let's clarify one important point: I'm not implying we shouldn't be "bold" in our proclamations (although in light of passages like 1 Peter 3:15, "…do this with gentleness and respect," and Colossians 3:12, "clothe yourselves with compassion, kindness, humility, gentleness and patience," I believe we *always* need to be cautious in our teaching and speaking). Rather, I believe we need to be as "shrewd as snakes and gentle as doves" (Matthew 10:16) in our responsibilities as God's chosen representatives of his truth.

The majority of adolescents who've been forced to listen to adults "communicate" with them throughout their lives will come into a meeting or program already convinced that the adult who holds the power is not all that concerned about who they are, what they think, and what matters to them. For that reason, many kids turn our messages off be-

DEEP MINISTRY

fore we even begin. Sure, they'll listen to our stories—but if we're not careful to connect with who they are and what they care about, then when we get to our appeal, they'll shut us out without giving us much of a chance.

∞ **DEEP DESIGN PROMPT**

Experience: Maybe in our zeal to be bold we've lost our calling to be respectful and shrewd.

Principle 3: God Is the One Who Transforms; Our Job Is to Help Him Plow the Field

In communicating the message of Christ, our efforts to persuade may stir others' souls and even contribute to changing their minds about something. But don't forget, we never actually change anyone. Any lasting transformation happens because God has done a work in the life of a believer who trusts him. As the apostle Paul writes, "But by faith *we eagerly await through the Spirit* the righteousness for which we hope" (Galatians 5:5, emphasis added). Ultimately, the Holy Spirit is the one who creates lasting change in the direction of holiness within the believer. Our role is to work with the Spirit's movement in someone's soul in order to create a willingness to respond.

∞ **DEEP DESIGN PROMPT**

Scripture: It is God who changes lives, and we work with him to prepare the soil.

With this in mind, there are three things we can do in our ministries to foster a willingness and openness to hear God's voice.

1. We must get kids into the Bible themselves instead of spoon-feeding them or trying to "wow" them with clever delivery systems.

2. We must prepare well so we have something solid and compelling to bring to the table. Last-minute or shoddy preparation leading to pooled ignorance will kill any Bible study.

3. As valuable and useful as they are, alternative and "creative" teaching methods can distract youth from focusing on the issues at hand. It's important to make sure that anything we use—object lessons, role plays, video clips, even cool illustrations from

when we were in high school—are *supplementary* to the content of the message. Our job is to create an atmosphere of dialogue and inquiry. Let *ideas* and *truth* provide the struggle and energy in our communication, whether it's speaking or teaching or facilitating a group.

HELPING STUDENTS TO HEAR GOD'S VOICE...

- Get them into the Bible
- Prepare well
- Keep "creative" teaching/speaking tools secondary to your message

---

8.6

Finally, remember that the most crucial element in communicating effectively with youth is believing so deeply in what you have to say and why it matters that it pours out of you naturally. You may never be a great speaker or have the funniest stories or hippest video presentations, but if you care—really care—about Jesus Christ and what he has to say to students, you will be a powerful communicator.

∞ **DEEP DESIGN PROMPT**

STEP 1: NOW?   **STEP 3: WHO?**

STEP 4: HOW?   STEP 2: NEW?

DEEP DESIGN, STEP 3 (OBSERVATION): *WHO?*

Jim Candy, director of middle school ministries at First Presbyterian Church in Boulder, Colorado, has been working with students for 10 years. Not only is Jim a great communicator, but he also understands how to connect with kids in ways that partner with God to bring lasting transformation. Here's what he has to say about communicating to students in ways that bring change:

Jim, I know much of your communication is influenced by what you call "associative value." What do you mean by that phrase?

If kids take away the idea that "Jim loves Jesus" from my talks, they will begin to associate me (and our leaders) with the person of Jesus.

That is huge in making relational ministry happen—it frames our relationships with them. Conversations with kids about their faith are priceless, but even if we don't get there, the fact that they associate us with Jesus, and we genuinely love and care for them, points them to Jesus.

Some youth workers feel the days of the youth ministry "talk" are dead or at least dying. What do you think?

I've talked to some middle school directors who have given up on talks because their kids don't respond verbally to the message. If nothing else, the associative factor they lose makes that a big mistake in my book.

Perfect example: I took an eighth grader named Clark fly-fishing with me one day during my first year. We laughed, caught fish, and never talked about God. Now, he's a leader for us, and in his story of how he came to follow Jesus, he talks about that day specifically because we *didn't* talk about God. He kept expecting me to bring up the "God talk," but because I didn't, he thought, "Maybe Jim just likes me." And the next step, "Maybe God just likes me, too."

Even though we didn't talk about God that day, he had heard me talk about Christ and associated me with him. If I hadn't been giving talks, I don't know that Clark would have made the cognitive leap of connecting my no-agenda, genuine love of him with God's love.

Jim, what are some ways you connect with kids when teaching or speaking?

I remind myself that connecting with kids doesn't begin when I get up and open my mouth. Engaging with kids in everything we do during the night leading up to the talk may help me connect more than anything I say during the talk itself.

The point was impressed on me a few years ago when Sean Matthews, an area director for Young Life in Denver, spoke at one of our summer camps. Sean was phenomenal. Kids were more tuned into Sean than any speaker I've seen.

At the end of the week, a seventh grader named Harry told his mom Sean was the best speaker he'd ever heard and that he was going to follow Jesus because of Sean. Harry's mom asked what Sean said that was so persuasive. "Um…I can't remember," he said. "But he played kickball with me."

Okay, but what about during the actual "talk" itself?

Connecting with kids during talks means being honest, genuine, transparent, and humble. I try to be the person God made me and be someone who shares with kids more than speaks at them.

On a practical note, I talk with groups of kids about my talk before I actually sit down and figure out what I'm going to say. Kids get excited about being included, I get an idea of what they actually think about the topic, and God often surprises me

by using those conversations to move kids or myself toward Jesus.

How do you know when you're effective? How can you tell? How do you measure it?

My ineffective talks are when I try to do too much rather than sticking to one great idea and developing it. I think this is a problem many of us get into—we're so excited about what we have to say that we put the dump truck in reverse and unload it on kids. To combat that tendency, we have the "minivan rule" in our ministry. The goal is that when a kid hops in their car at the end of the night and someone asks, "What did they talk about tonight?" the kid can articulate in a sentence what the point of the night was. It forces us to be clear, concise, and know exactly what we're trying to communicate.

How much do you base your feelings of effectiveness on feedback you get from students and leaders?

Obviously I listen closely to what people have to say, but I'm careful not to base my feelings of effectiveness on how kids immediately respond to a talk. We can deliver great messages, not get a single encouraging word from kids or leaders, and go home feeling like failures. The advantage of being in youth ministry for the long haul is hearing former students come back and tell you about a talk you gave that was important to their faith development. I'm often surprised that some of the talks I thought were disasters were the ones God chose to use.

How do you (and your team) use and incorporate creative tools and resources (media, illustrations, role plays, drama, etc.)?

We use PowerPoint®, video, and dramas, but the best creative tools support an overall goal of connecting with kids on a more personal level. I don't have time to go over the top with media presentations—otherwise I'll never spend time with kids and leaders. I never want fancy media to be the focus. But it's always paid off when I've prepared a slide show that depicts my home and family or a funny home video of my boys—often there are ways to tie in that type of media with whatever idea you present and, in the process, build a bond between yourself and kids. Illustrations like that let kids into your life—and kids desperately need to be let in.

∞ DEEP DESIGN PROMPT

STEP 1: NOW?   STEP 3: WHO?

STEP 4: HOW?   STEP 2: NEW?

DEEP DESIGN, STEP 4 (APPLICATION): *HOW?*

Application Questions:

1. What is your greatest strength as a communicator? What is your greatest weakness?

2. When you're speaking or teaching, what's the balance between grabbing (and keeping) attention and getting to the point? How do you find that balance?

3. This chapter talks about Social Judgment Theory. Where have you seen this in your ministry? Compare those times when you've experienced students invested and engaged in a Bible study and when they've been either bored or defensive/dismissive. What contributed to these reactions?

4. How is your situation similar to Jim's? How is it different?

5. Given all this reflection on communication, how can you go deeper?

How are we going to go deeper in our communication?	Source

CHAPTER 9

DEEP MISSIONS: WHY ARE SO FEW KIDS INTERESTED IN SERVICE AND MISSIONS?

Kara Powell

DEEP DESIGN, STEP 1 (DISCERNMENT): *NOW?*

How could he get his 14-year-old son to be grateful for all their family had? How could he help Curtis see the extent of poverty and how it affects people near and far?

Curtis' dad decided the best way to open his son's eyes to the contrast between how much their family had and how little most of the world had was to take him on a weekend service trip. Along with six others from their church, Curtis and his dad spent two days serving a rural family who lived on a farm in their county. They did whatever needed to be done—from milking cows to painting barn walls to (you guessed it) cleaning up after the horses.

As they drove back home on Sunday night, Curtis' dad asked his son, "What did you think of the trip?"

"It was great."

"Did you see how poor people can be?"

"You bet."

"What did you learn?"

"I saw that we have one dog at home, and they have four. We have a pool that reaches to the middle of the garden; they have a creek that has no end. We have imported lamps in the garden; they have the stars. Our patio reaches to the front yard; they have a whole horizon."

The father was speechless. After a few seconds, Curtis added, "Thanks, Dad, for showing me how poor we are."

Given the story I've just shared, you might guess that I'm biased when it comes to mission trips. And you'd be right. I love mission trips. If a student is able to attend only one youth ministry event in a summer and wants my opinion about what it should be, I'll point the student toward a one-week trip to Mexico. Mission trips combine all the

great dynamics of sweeping kids away from "normal life" (just like retreats and camps) PLUS chances to grow as they interact with those in different communities and from different backgrounds.

I'm also biased because of the significant role mission trips have played in my own life. I met my husband on a mission trip. We got engaged on a mission trip. (No, not the same trip!) One year into our marriage, we signed and faxed legal documents to purchase our first house while serving together on a mission trip. Other than the births of our two children, most of the significant events in our marriage have been somehow connected to cross-cultural service.

Whether you're 15 or 55, there's something intrinsically powerful about being in a different and unfamiliar context. Whether it's a Saturday morning at the local children's hospital, a weekend with an inner-city homeless ministry, or a week in Zambia serving children affected by HIV/AIDS, mission trips offer opportunities to deepen our conceptions of life, God, and people. We realize our corner of the world is actually pretty tiny, and the world itself is actually pretty enormous.

In the midst of all of our "good" service trips, every once in a while, we'd end up with a truly great trip. Students shared everything with one another—from pesos to prayer requests. The boundary between who was giving and who was receiving was jumbled as the high school students from our group and members of the community we were visiting served one another. The students' comments about how they were affected transcended the more typical statements about being "grateful for all I have" and focused instead on being "grateful for the God I serve."

What separates a "good" service or mission event from a "great" one? What allows "good trip memories" to be-

∞ DEEP DESIGN PROMPT
Creating space for God's transformation: Being in different and unfamiliar contexts.

∞ DEEP DESIGN PROMPT
Creating space for God's transformation: Service and mission trips come in different shapes and formats.

∞ DEEP DESIGN PROMPT
Creating space for God's transformation: Service and mission trips stretch our view of the world.

∞ DEEP DESIGN PROMPT
Creating space for God's transformation: Most trips are good.

∞ DEEP DESIGN PROMPT
Hindering God's transformation: Few trips are truly great.

come "great life change"? We are often so busy preparing and packing for trips **Now** that we never stop to ask and answer those questions. By checking out the **New** findings of other researchers and youth workers, we can wrestle with these questions until we pin down some satisfying answers.

STEP 1: NOW?　STEP 3: WHO?

STEP 4: HOW?　**STEP 2: NEW?**

Research: Great mission trips have a much bigger sense of "calendar."

Research: Mission trips have three time phases—before, during, and after.

DEEP DESIGN, STEP 2 (REFLECTION): *NEW?*

If you've ever planned a mission trip, you probably followed some basic steps. Figure out where you want to go. Develop a plan for what you'll do there. Work out logistics like food, housing, and transportation. Come up with some way to pay for it all. Encourage students and adults to sign up. Mix it all together, and you've got yourself a pretty decent trip.

But if you want a great trip, you're probably going to need a whole **New** missions calendar. Most of the ingredients I listed above relate to the two days or two weeks you're gone. Deeper mission trips require a much larger sense of "calendar."

Most youth workers tend to think of a mission trip in a single phase: the trip. **New** research suggests we need to expand our view of trips into three time phases: *before* the trip, *during* the trip, and *after* the trip.

BEFORE	DURING	AFTER

9.1

If you're planning a one-week trip to an urban area two hours away, your time frame might look something like this:

BEFORE	DURING	AFTER
Three months	One week	Three months

9.2

If you're planning a three-hour visit to the local homeless shelter, your time frame might look more like this:

BEFORE	DURING	AFTER
One hour	Three hours	One hour

9.3

No matter the length of our service or missions events, we will go deeper if we recalibrate our calendars to think in terms of three phases, not just one.

Why all that "extra" time?
The primary reason for the additional time is quite simple: it's mainly to give our students time and space to process what they're experiencing.

Imagine yourself and a vanload of students on a Saturday Service Blitz for the senior citizens of your church. Five different seniors contacted you the month before your Saturday event with needs ranging from moving boxes to raking leaves. The fifth house was further from the church than you realized, so now you're not sure you're going to make it back on time. Given that you were 10 minutes late returning from last month's Saturday Service Blitz (and parents are still ticked about it), you know you're going to get some angry stares if you pull into the parking lot late again.

You'd planned to sit down with the kids over blended mochas on the way back to church and ask them what they thought and felt about their time serving. But now you have a choice: you get back to church on time, or you sit and talk about your service.

The thought of the parental glares makes the choice easy. You speed past the coffee shop and head back to church, thinking maybe you can lead a discussion while driving. You crane your head toward the back of the van and ask, "So, what did you guys think of what we did today?"

A few students answer, "It was cool."

"I liked it."

"The cookies at that last house were great."

Trying to take it a bit deeper, you say something like, "I'm really proud of you for how you served today. Jesus was the ultimate servant, and when we serve, we reflect him to others."

You're wondering if anyone is going to comment further, or if you need to ask a question when the decision is made for you—from the back of the van someone says,

"Oh, man, I hate that pizza place we just passed. Last time I ate there my sister got sick and threw up all over our table."

Multiple moans of, "Eww, gross," as students try to top that story with their own vomit tales, told in 3-D detail.

The golden moment is gone. There's no way to reclaim the conversation now. You didn't have much chance to process with the kids, but at least you're back to church on time.

∞ DEEP DESIGN PROMPT

Research: Reflection is the link between service and learning.

What did you end up with? A good (but not great) Saturday Service Blitz.

∞ DEEP DESIGN PROMPT

Scripture: Reflection is often a key step in our growth path.

We who want truly great service and mission trips have much to learn from the field of service-learning. Service-learning is a growing academic discipline that helps students learn from service as part of their coursework. One of the prominent service-learning researchers, Janet Eyler, writes, "Reflection is the hyphen that links service to learning."[61] As a follower of Christ, I would modify that to say *Holy Spirit-inspired reflection* is the link between service and learning. (See Chapter 12 on focus groups for more on the Holy Spirit.)

To read more about the latest research on service and short-term missions, check out a free resource at www. cyfm.net.

The Holy Spirit often uses reflection as a key step in our path to growth through service. From the wisdom of Peter at the Jerusalem Council in Acts 15 to the compelling power of Paul's speeches and reason in his journeys, we see that mental engagement is a major force in our spiritual development.

∞ DEEP DESIGN PROMPT

Research: We'd probably be better off doing less "work" and more reflection.

Looking back at the Saturday Service Blitz example, those students would probably have learned and grown more deeply if you had helped four seniors instead of five and spent that extra 45 minutes talking over blended mochas. Sure you would have accomplished less work.

[61] Janet Eyler, "Reflecting on Service: Helping Nursing Students Get the Most From Service-Learning," *Educational Innovations*, October 2002, Volume 41, no. 10, 453.

But if less work means more reflection and transformation, then put down that rake and take a seat with some kids.

Maybe you're already convinced of the importance of reflecting with students about their service, but you're not sure how to actually do it. A great way to help students process what they're experiencing is to follow one of Jesus' strategies and ask questions. Before, during, and after both major and minor episodes in his life with the disciples, Jesus often posed questions to help catalyze their thinking. In the midst of the Sermon on the Mount, he asks, "If the salt loses its saltiness, how can it be made salty again?" (Matthew 5:13). As the disciples feel threatened by a storm they think spells doom for their boat (and them!), Jesus asks, "You of little faith, why are you so afraid?" (Matthew 8:26). When he's alone with the disciples, he asks them, "Who do the crowds say I am?" and later, "Who do you say I am?" (Luke 9:18, 20).

In light of this chapter's topic, it's interesting to note that Jesus also uses questions in the midst of one of his supreme acts of service before his death. Just prior to the Passover Feast, Jesus gathers with his disciples for dinner. No servants are present, and none of Jesus' disciples volunteered for the lowly task of foot washing, as they would be considered inferior to all the others. So Jesus volunteers. When he finishes, he puts on his clothes, returns to his place, and asks, "Do you understand what I have done for you?" (John 13:12). While Jesus goes on to provide the answer himself, his question must have gotten the disciples' mental juices flowing.

The questions you ask students to consider don't have to be complex. One very effective way to get your kids

reflecting on a service opportunity is by asking three simple questions:

1. What?

2. So what?

3. Now what?

The beauty of this three-question reflection is that it helps students move from shallowness to depth by jumping from the tangible to the abstract and from the general to the specific.[62] By asking "What?" students have a chance to talk about what they actually saw, heard, smelled, and felt. In asking "So what?" students have the opportunity to think about the difference this experience can make in their lives. By reflecting upon "Now what?" students can think about how they want to live, act, or be different when they return to their so-called "normal" lives.

If you're serving with students who struggle to process their feelings or experiences (can anyone say "middle school boys"?), then you may get just a few morsels of conversation at first. Answers may range from "I don't know" to "What he said." That's okay. Sometimes it's taken me months—even years—to get to the point where students are able to truly join in the reflection. With some students we never got to the point of truly deep conversation. But I've tried to model patient listening and simply being there with them in the meantime.

Reflection is something that should happen before, during, and after your mission trips. The following chart should give you **New** ideas on how you can use *What? So what? Now what?* to facilitate truly great discussions with your own students.

---

[62] The Campus Outreach Opportunity League has popularized this three-question reflection exercise.

Phase One: Before the Trip

DISCUSSION TOPIC	WHAT? SO WHAT? NOW WHAT? QUESTIONS
HOPES	1. What hopes do you have about our trip?
	2. So what do these hopes say about you and your view of service?
	3. Now what can you do to make sure your hopes are realized?
FEARS	1. What fears do you have about this trip?
	2. So what do your fears say about you and your view of service?
	3. Now what can you do to make sure you address and even overcome your fears?
TEAM DYNAMICS	1. What type of relationships do we want to have on our team?
	2. Given that, so what are some ways we need to treat each other?
	3. Now what can we do to make sure we treat each other those ways?
SPIRITUAL GIFTS & ABILITIES	1. What are your spiritual gifts and abilities?
	2. So what are some ways you can use your gifts and abilities during your service?
	3. Now what can you do to maximize your gifts?
CULTURAL ISSUES	1. What are some ways the people we're serving are different than we are?
	2. So what should we do while we're around them to honor and serve them well?
	3. Now what can we do to prepare ourselves to be around those who are different?

9.4

Phase Two: During the Trip

DISCUSSION TOPIC	WHAT? SO WHAT? NOW WHAT? QUESTIONS
HIGHS & LOWS	1. What was the best and worst part of the service for you?
	2. So what have you learned from these highs and lows?
	3. Now what should you do differently when you get back?
FEELINGS	1. What about the experience made you mad, glad, sad, or scared?
	2. So what caused you to feel that way?
	3. Based on your feelings, now what are some steps you should be taking?
GOD SIGHTINGS	1. What did you see that was clearly of God?
	2. So what caused it to make such an impression on you?
	3. Now what difference do you want this to make in your life?
LEARNING FROM THE COMMUNITY	1. What did you learn from those you served?
	2. So what makes that significant for you?
	3. Now what difference do you want it to make in how you treat others?

9.5

Phase Three: After the Trip

RESOURCES — MONEY & TIME	1. Based on what you experienced, what do you think you should be doing with your resources, like your money and time?
	2. So what would be different if you did that?
	3. Now what would you like to do about it this week or this month?
RELATIONSHIPS	1. What did you learn about relationships as you served?
	2. So what makes this insight important to you?
	3. Now what are some ways you'd like to treat others differently?
THE WORLD	1. What are some insights you gleaned about the world around you?
	2. So what makes these insights important to you?
	3. Now what are some ways you'd like to view, treat, or interact with the world differently?

9.6

These conversations could take 15 minutes, or they could take two hours. In general, the shorter your service experience, the shorter your time of reflection.

Sometimes circumstances make it impossible to wrangle enough reflection time. Occasionally we don't budget our time well. Even the best-laid plans fall prey to unexpected traffic jams or broken-down vans. When (note I say "when," not "if") that happens, look for other opportunities in the next few weeks to try to process the experience with kids. Whether in person at church or during small group, or over the phone or e-mail, even just asking the simple question, "What memories of our service are most vivid for you?" can help those experiences leave a more lasting impression.

DEEP DESIGN PROMPT

Experience: We're often unsure if anyone other than our students have benefited.

From catching fish for them to teaching them to fish

There's a common, sometimes subconscious, belief that when it comes to mission trips, it's more about what our students learn than how those we serve are changed. When I ask youth pastors about recent mission trips, they often make statements like, "It was GREAT for our kids, and I think we helped the people there at least a little bit."

I want trips to change our students' lives. But I also think it's our responsibility to maximize the changes in the people we serve. It's not enough to "hope we do more good than harm" when we go to Mexico or the dump in Guatemala City.

DEEP DESIGN PROMPT

Research: Deeper mission means capacity-building.

It's relatively easy to swarm around a construction site for four days and leave a 300-square-foot house for a family that used to huddle each night in a cardboard shack. It's much harder to view that four-day trip as a chance not just to serve but also to build the capacity of that family so they can keep improving their situations.

Rich Lerner from Tufts University suggests a New developmental paradigm that helps youth groups deepen the capacity of people they serve. According to Lerner, empowering others involves increasing their:

- Competence in academic, social, emotional, and vocational arenas;

- Confidence in who they are becoming;

- Connection to others;

- Character and a strong sense of values and morals; and

- Caring and compassion.[63]

∞ DEEP DESIGN PROMPT

Research: We can build capacity by increasing their competency, confidence, connection, character, caring, and contributions.

Another researcher, Karen Pittman, suggests there is a sixth "C": **Contribution** to their families, neighbors, and community.[64]

If you want to apply these "Six Cs" to go deeper with your next service event or mission trip, here are some **New** ideas:

Competence: Instead of acting like a posse of benevolent Santa Clauses who unload gifts and treats from your fleet of minivans, involve those you're serving in whatever activities you're coordinating. Ask them to make decisions with you. If you're short on paintbrushes, give them yours and cheer them on as they improve their own community.

Confidence: Instead of viewing yourselves as group of Divine Supermen and Superwomen who "rescue" others from a life of misery and hardship, try affirming all they are already doing to benefit their own lives and communities. Discuss with them a vision and strategy for how they can continue to shape their community after you leave. Recognizing with them how much they've

[63] Rich M. Lerner, *Adolescence: Development, Diversity, Context, and Application* (Upper Saddle River, NJ: Prentice Hall, 2002).

[64] Karen J. Pittman, "Balancing the Equation: Communities Supporting Youth, Youth Supporting Communities," *Community Youth Development Journal*, 1, 2000, 33-36.

overcome to create what order and beauty there is in their environment will help.

Connection: Instead of just connecting with one group, your arrival might serve as an opportunity to work with other churches, ministries, and nonprofit organizations they normally don't talk to. Invite other local leaders to join together in hosting a children's recreation day or a special dinner for the community. Your presence and intentional invitations might convene partners who would otherwise remain isolated.

Character: Instead of helping only with the physical needs in the community you serve, think ahead of time about what you can do to strengthen the morals and integrity of those you serve. Maybe you could study the fruits of the spirit together or discuss various leaders in Scripture who learned how to trust in God's faithfulness in the midst of life's roller coasters.

Caring: Instead of you doing 100 percent of the caring and serving, identify ways your hosts can care for you in return. Perhaps they could cook you a meal or provide snacks in the middle of the day. Instead of you leading the worship time at the end of the day, allow them to minister to you through their own worship, music, and art.

Contribution: Try to make it clear that you want to learn from them also. Your trip should reflect mutual giving and receiving, so that all experience the dignity that comes from being a partner, not a beggar. You might have some construction expertise and the finances to buy the soccer balls and tacos, but you are in their hometown as their guests and need their hospitality in many ways.

From teaching them to fish to helping them own the pond

If you're interested in building the capacity of those you serve in even deeper ways, then it's time to think about *community* capacity-building so your service won't be needed a decade from now. As seen in the diagram below, you move beyond teaching others how to fish for themselves to empowering others to build and own the pond.[65]

∞ DEEP DESIGN PROMPT

Research: True capacity-building helps them not just fish for themselves, but own the pond.

CAPACITY-BUILDING CONTINUUM

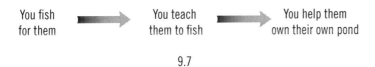

You fish for them → You teach them to fish → You help them own their own pond

9.7

This type of large-scale capacity building is not something that can be done in one trip, or even in one year. It takes multiple visits over a number of years and is probably best accomplished if you team up with other youth ministries or groups in your own church. It means you don't just bring down doctors for a week and leave medical supplies, but you help the community set up its own health center. You don't just encourage other businesses to invest in the community, but you help the people come up with their own business plans and start their own local businesses. Such efforts take plenty of blood, sweat, tears, and TIME—but if you feel God leading you deeper in your service and mission trips, you won't regret it.

[65] DeVos Urban Leadership Initiative, Notes from Workshop 21, Spring 2005.

DEEP DESIGN, STEP 3 (OBSERVATION): WHO?

Sandy Moy Liu has been pastor of youth and children at Chinese Bible Church of Greater Boston for the last 16 years. She has developed a deep missions philosophy and program that involves more than 50 students annually. Whether her students are serving locally in inner-city Boston, cross-culturally at Native American reservations, or overseas in Asia, she creatively structures her ministry calendar to give plenty of time for students' preparation and debriefing, as well as focusing on building the capacity of those they serve.

What impact has mission work had on your kids?

By God's grace, students who have gone on our mission trips are fervent in their walks with Christ, give to missions when they become adults, and sometimes even work overseas after they graduate. It's so moving to me when some of my graduates of top colleges choose to work and serve in Asia, Europe, or Africa because they recognize the great needs outside of the United States. They say part of their desire to serve overseas sprang from their experiences in our youth group.

What type of training do you provide for your trips?

Our training is pretty extensive. For five months prior to the trip, we send them into an elective Mission Sunday school class to understand a biblical perspective on missions, how to share their faith, and cultural issues they'll encounter. During class breakouts, our specific teams include students in logistical decisions about what we'll do and how we'll do it, so the students own the trip. We may

also have one or two overnight lock-ins for each team for bonding and preparation. Those have been mini-simulations of what we'll be doing on the actual trip. To prepare our Hopi Mission team to rough it in tents in the open Arizona desert, we pitched tents in the church lobby overnight. We also run through whatever dramas, games, or programs we'll be doing on the actual trips, so kids feel more comfortable with their roles.

Five months and multiple overnighters is a big commitment for a high school kid. Do students try to get out of coming to the training events?

Not usually. We give them plenty of goof-off time during the training and retreats, so they actually look forward to it. We spiritually challenge one another to pray diligently for the trip and our life concerns in general. Kids enjoy getting tight with their team.

Often parents are the ones who are hesitant to let their kids make such commitments because they're concerned about their kids' busyness, or homework, or they just don't want to have to keep driving them to meetings. How do parents respond to what you're asking of their kids?

At the first meeting, students are challenged to sign up for a mission team only if they can give it top priority among all their activities. Some have given up sports or music lessons or school clubs to focus on the mission. Especially in my culture, this is a family decision, not a personal decision. Our church believes in family missions, not merely youth missions.

It's been super-encouraging seeing God work on parents' hearts. Some who were initially resistant have ended up in tears and said things like, "We see the power of God working in our children, and we feel honored now."

How do you think the fact that your kids and families are primarily Asian affects their willingness to make that commitment?

It's definitely a factor, but it's more than just an ethnically based willingness to work hard. It took us years to create the type of missions culture we have in our youth ministry. In the early years we were mostly planting seeds with kids, parents, and church leaders. We'd have only a few training meetings and maybe one or two parent meetings, and that was it.

How do you choose where to serve?

The key for us is developing a true partnership with the site and its leaders. We try to go back year after year to the same sites. That way we really get to know the people there as well as the local church leaders. We stay in touch with them during the year through e-mail, letters, and phone calls. We're especially committed to encouraging those in the community to be grounded in their local churches, so that's a constant theme in our communication with them. When the local kids and families grow in their faith and lead others in their community to Christ, we feel like our mission is successful. It may take years or decades to see these prayers answered.

In research language, we call that "building capacity." What else do you do to build the capacity of those communities?

We leave them all sorts of resources. If they need books, we bring them books. If they need sports equipment, we leave them every piece of equipment we bring down with us. We've left guitars, CDs, Bibles, and anything else useful to further their local ministry.

Often what these communities need is vision. A few years ago, we worked with youth in a London church that had a pretty small vision for how God could use them. They felt ill-equipped and unqualified. Working with a local mission agency, we encouraged them to think about reaching out to others in Europe—and after we left, their youth group actually did it. So here is this group from Boston that somehow mobilized a group in London, who in turn is spreading the gospel throughout Europe. To me, when the "mission field" becomes the "mission senders," that's the ultimate form of capacity-building.

How do you debrief your trips?

Our ideal adult-to-student ratio is to have one adult for every four or five students, both for mentoring and supervision. During the trips, we hold hour-long daily debriefings and prayer with small groups of students. Students give and receive feedback, refocusing, kudos, and support during these daily times.

At the end of the trip, the team spends two days in intensive fun and thorough debriefing. We ask questions such as *What are the best things we learned or witnessed on our mission? What could have been better? What did each member of the team do well? What are some suggestions for each member of the team to serve even more effectively?* These are our deepest team moments when we all laugh and cry together. So much took place during the mission, and each of us sees a part of it. It's at the debriefing where all the pieces of the puzzle come together.

You're obviously very committed to preparing kids and debriefing with them for long trips. Do you also debrief your two-hour trips to inner-city Boston to feed the homeless?

We debrief *everything*! We ask questions afterward such as *what went well today? What was God doing? Did you see God doing what we thought he was going to do?* Actually, the question of trying to discern what God is doing is a theme in all of our preparation and debriefing, no matter what trip or event it is. We want our kids to have their internal radars tuned to try to figure out what God is up to.

We also make sure our students are heavily involved ahead of time. When we take kids to serve a meal at a homeless shelter, we meet with them a few weeks ahead of time to involve them in the preparation process. We ask them to help us figure out what food to serve, and why that food would be more suitable than other choices. Sure, it takes more time, but we see the results as our students take responsibility and leadership.

Your church must be pretty supportive of youth missions. What's made them so supportive?

God is merciful! After one particular parent-leader joined a team and was quite moved by the Lord, he became a positive influence and recruited other parents for missions. We've found that when several key leaders from the church become enthusiastically active in missions, the rest of the church is more likely to get on board.

When it comes to missions, what are you still trying to figure out?

You know, I still wrestle with a lot of deep questions about missions. *Why, Lord, is there so much global poverty and suffering when we Americans have so much? How can we Americans go and see others' spiritual and material needs, and then come home and go back to life as normal?* These are tough questions, and I don't have any easy answers.

What would you say to encourage someone who wants to help students go deep in missions but isn't sure how to start?

Pray with your students, and listen for God's calling. Help your students develop hearts for the lost and a passion for sharing the gospel. Hold a few training meetings and a few hours of debriefing. Then in the future, perhaps add a few additional training and debriefing opportunities.

Missions is much more than merely a "trip"; it's a real-life laboratory for our faith. God's work has exceeded even our biggest dreams, and he'll work in your ministry, too.

DEEP DESIGN, STEP 4 (APPLICATION): *HOW?*

Application Questions:

1. How have mission trips and service events helped you or your students grow deeper in the past?

2. What do you think of the suggestion of debriefing by asking *What? So what?* and *Now what?* How might you use those questions in your next trip or activity?

3. Which of the "Six Cs" do you think you could focus on in your next service event or mission trip? What would you gain by doing that? What would you lose?

4. When you look at the Capacity-Building Continuum on page 185, where do you think you fall? What could you do to move further to the right?

5. How is your ministry similar to Sandy's? How is it different?

6. What can you apply from this chapter and Sandy's story to take your service and ministry to a deeper level?

How are we going to go deeper in our service and missions?	Source

CHAPTER 10
DEEP WORSHIP:
WHO ARE STUDENTS
BECOMING WHEN WE
LEAD THEM IN WORSHIP?

Kara Powell and Brad Griffin

Brad Griffin is project manager for the Center for Youth and Family Ministry at Fuller Theological Seminary. Brad has been involved in youth and worship ministry for the last 10 years in Kentucky, Illinois, and southern California, and is now an M.Div. student at Fuller. He lives in Pasadena with his wife and two daughters.

DEEP DESIGN, STEP 1 (DISCERNMENT): *NOW?*

"The question before us…is not *whether* our people will learn when they worship. The question is, *What* will they learn when we lead them in worship?"[66]

We wish we could stamp this quote by theologian and author Will Willimon on every youth ministry's order of service, every music leader's guitar, and every church's worship bulletin.

Let's be honest: for most of us, worship means the right words, the right prayers, the right music, done the right way, by the right musicians, with the right multimedia trimmings. "Deeper" worship **Now** means having a student band that actually practices or even—gasp!—chooses songs that fit the theme of the service. What would it mean to take our worship—our music, our prayers, our rituals, and our interactions with Scripture—into **New** and more life-giving waters?

Brad will start with his own confession and crisis as a worship leader:

A few years into ministry, I found myself wondering from time to time after a song or a prayer, *Do I actually believe that?* One song in particular, "At the Cross," sticks out in my mind.[67] A former youth pastor had taught our group the lines, "At the cross, he died for our sins. At the cross, he gave his life again." Every time we sang those lyrics, the word *again* slapped me in the face. *Again?* I wrestled with this theology, BUT KEPT SINGING IT. Even worse, I was the guy with the guitar and the microphone, leading the "student band" as we, in turn, led the kids and adults in worship.

Finally (after a couple of years—I'm not kidding!) I tracked down the real words. To my great relief, I found that the original read, "He gave *us* life again"! Big differ-

---

[66] William H. Willimon, *Worship as Pastoral Care*, (Nashville: Abingdon, 1979), 122-123.
[67] Randy Butler and Terry Butler, ©1993 Mercy/Vineyard Publishing.

ence. Looking back, I wonder…*what did those students think about themselves and their sins, sending Jesus to the cross again and again? Was once not enough? Were students learning that the cross didn't really make that much of an impact, or that it was just one of many ways God had to give his life for our sins?*

What about you? Have you ever edited a line like "Holiness is what you want from me"[68] to read "Holiness is what you want for me"? There's some theological distance between those pleas worth considering.

The problem goes deeper than song lyrics. I've seen from my own leadership how shallow and puny our worship can be when we thoughtlessly "wing it" from week to week. At times it can even be contra-transformational.

Chew on that for a minute.

Contra-transformational.

In the end, our shallowness cheats God and kids.

If we're not careful, communal worship **Now** can reinforce unhealthy leadership models, introduce destructive practices and processes into worshipers' lives, or help maintain a denial of reality by feeding escapist mentalities.[69] When all of our songs and prayers are based on transporting us to hyperindividual states of spiritual oneness with God, we are likely to miss out on the distinctly *communal* nature of worship. This individual focus might also cheat the biblical imperatives to care for the people and world around us as an extension of our worship (see Isaiah 58).

Worship can also become a tool of oppression when leaders see it as an opportunity to control others or push their own agendas. This can happen in any number of ways: urging the manipulation of certain spiritual gifts to

∞ DEEP DESIGN PROMPT

Creating space for God's transformation: Causing us to rethink what students are learning during worship.

∞ DEEP DESIGN PROMPT

Hindering God's transformation: Shallow worship can be contra-transformational.

∞ DEEP DESIGN PROMPT

Hindering God's transformation: Sometimes our worship teaches students the wrong messages.

---

[68] "Take My Life," Scott Underwood, ©1995 Mercy/Vineyard Publishing.
[69] Willimon, *Worship as Pastoral Care*, 63.

prove the presence of the Holy Spirit; submerging genuine expression of the same; or modeling a one-man/woman-show approach to leadership (haven't we had enough of that?).

Without thoughtful preparation, even our best attempts at "spontaneity" can come across as if we don't really care about what we're doing. Or worse, they can communicate that we think God doesn't really care about what we're doing. Perhaps we should think twice before tossing the keys to our student band and saying, "You plan it, you lead it." When we do we're saying, in effect, "It doesn't matter all that much." Not that student-led worship is always bad, but is it really transformative when we abandon 16-year-olds to create a worship plan based on what songs they *like* this week?

Maybe it's time for us to get beyond how-to manuals for putting worship teams together or designing "engaging" worship services for students. Maybe it's time for us to rethink the direction our worship is heading. If we're not careful, we could be singing ourselves—and the students under our care—nowhere.

DEEP DESIGN, STEP 2 (REFLECTION): *NEW?*

Worship is more than a certain kind of music, more than what happens in the church sanctuary on Sunday mornings. For that matter, worship is more than a "worship service." Paul reminds us that our "everyday, walking-around, going-to-school-and-work lives" are by their nature created as acts of worship and living sacrifices offered to God (Romans 12:1-2, adapted from *The Message*). In the midst of our lifestyle of worship, specific gatherings for worship lead us into a mysterious interaction with God—a holy dialogue—and we should expect to come out of it transformed in some way. When we lead adolescents into

a worship encounter, what do we expect will happen to them? *Anything?*

I'd like to suggest that identity formation is one of the transformative processes that takes place through the mystery of worship. Identity formation is not the goal—worshiping God is—but nevertheless it's something that happens *to* us and *in* us when we worship.

At the heart of the human experience, we want to know who we are, why we exist, and how we relate to others. We yearn to live meaningfully; we long to discover what—and whose—story we are part of. These issues are especially present and powerful during adolescence. A multidisciplinary area of research and speculation, identity formation has recently reemerged as a significant focus of study in the social sciences. For those who work among adolescents within the context of the church, paying attention to what psychology, sociology, and anthropology say about identity development may result in a **New** understanding of the adolescent journey.

The process of identity formation in adolescents is closely linked to the task of *individuation*. Individuation involves developing into a distinct person, separate from the childhood roles in the family system. During individuation, a person develops the ability to interact healthily within and outside those relationships of origin, becoming part of a larger community. Using the metaphor of a tightrope walk, Chap frames the adolescent task of individuation through three critical questions: "Who am I?" (identity), "Do I matter?" (autonomy), and "How do I relate to others?" (belonging/reconnection).[70] Each child walks the tightrope of adolescence from childhood toward adulthood, desperately needing mature adults to be both guides and safety nets.

∞ **DEEP DESIGN PROMPT**

Scripture: Worship is more than music or just a "worship service"; worship is a lifestyle.

∞ **DEEP DESIGN PROMPT**

Experience: Our identity is formed as we worship God.

∞ **DEEP DESIGN PROMPT**

Research: Individuation is an experience revolving around identity, autonomy, and belonging.

---

[70] Chap Clark, "The Changing Face of Adolescence: A Theological View of Human Development," *Starting Right*, ed. Kenda C. Dean, Chap Clark, and Dave Rahn, (Grand Rapids: Zondervan, 2001), 47-55.

Historically, Erik Erikson was the first "guru" of identity development. He designated seven life stages of identity formation, labeling *crisis* and *decision* as the means through which individuals progress through the stages. In Erikson's model, adolescence is marked by the resolution of the crisis of *identity* versus *identity/role confusion.*[71] Erikson believed that navigating this transition leads to the adolescent's developing a sense of individuality, a role in society, an experience of continuity across time, and a commitment to ideals.[72] To add to the complexity of this task, adolescents often carry all kinds of unresolved crises from earlier stages of identity formation, including feelings of mistrust, shame, guilt, and inferiority.[73]

The power of a person's family, peers, broader community, and culture in helping to resolve these issues is undeniable. Teenagers often find that their identities are associated and strengthened by some sort of medium: "an object, an act, a music, an art, a language, a banner that serves as a label, insignia…These tag a human group and…in turn assume the identity of the group."[74]

So human identity development seems to involve some level of personal discovery, interaction with others in the context of a larger narrative, and communication through cultural symbol or ritual.

As youth workers, we often try to help students understand their identities by turning to Scripture. Scripture and the Christian faith are unambiguous regarding the question of human identity: we were created in the image of God (Genesis 1:26-27) so that our very existence reveals God's glory. Henri Nouwen proposes that true identity is discovered as we hear the voice of God calling us *beloved.* The words "You are my beloved" reveal "the most intimate truth about all human beings."[75]

∞ DEEP DESIGN PROMPT

Research: Adolescence is marked by the resolution of the crisis of identity versus identity/role confusion.

∞ DEEP DESIGN PROMPT

Research: Identity development involves personal discovery, interaction with others, and cultural symbols and rituals.

∞ DEEP DESIGN PROMPT

Scripture: Our identities as humans are rooted in the image of God.

[71] Erik H. Erikson, *Identity and the Life Cycle*, (New York: W.W. Norton Co., 1959, 1980).

[72] David Moshman, *Adolescent Psychological Development: Rationality, Morality, and Identity* (London: Lawrence Erlbaum Associates, 1999), 70.

[73] Erik H. Erikson, *Identity: Youth and Crisis* (New York: W.W. Norton, 1968, 1994).

[74] Adelaida Reyes, "Identity, Diversity, and Interaction", *The Garland Encyclopedia of World Music*, Vol. III: *The United States and Canada*, ed. Ellen Koskoff, (New York: Garland, 2001), 505.

[75] Henri Nouwen, *Life of the Beloved: Spiritual Living in a Secular World* (New York: Crossroad, 1992), 30.

Worship is a prime opportunity for us to realize our be-loved-ness. The God we worship not only created us in his image, but also *re*-creates us by Christ's work of reconcili-ation (2 Corinthians 5) and names us as God's children (1 John 3:1-2).[76] Reflecting on God's redemption means we're *doing theology* when we worship. Even more than that, wor-ship becomes a *transformational acting-out of theology.*

∞ DEEP DESIGN PROMPT

History: True identity is discovered as we real-ize we are the beloved.

For kids, this transformation through worship happens on the deepest levels of reality: identity, autonomy, and be-longing. As adults who care about kids, we help guide stu-dents away from the cultural baggage they've accumulated and toward the heart of their God-created identity in Christ. We help foster worship environments that encourage stu-dents carefully across the bridge of adolescence into adult-hood alongside their families. We'll be better guides on this important journey of identity formation as we explore **New** ways that worship helps students navigate their experienc-es and relationships. Since no two communities share an identical landscape, your next step is to understand the hills and valleys of the unique contexts of your own kids.

Your Students' Contexts

The body of Christ is always located in a missional-con-textual reality.[77] In other words, while all Christian com-munities share much in common, each has its own distinct characteristics and nuances. Even savvy youth workers need to step back from time to time and take inventory of how their youth ministries are—or aren't—matching the real needs and issues of their students. A key question for us becomes: *how is God forming a new identity among this specific people, in this specific time and place?*

∞ DEEP DESIGN PROMPT

Experience: We all need to match our worship experiences against the needs and issues of our students.

[76] A quick skim through further Scriptures that speak to aspects of our identity as created by God and re-deemed by Christ: Deuteronomy 8:3; Job 38-41; Psalm 95:6-7; 100:3; 139; Matthew 5:13-16; John 1:12-13; 3:3-21; 10:3-8; 14:10-11; 17:21; Romans 5:1-11; 8:14-17; 1 Corinthians 3:16; 6:19; 12:12-31; 2 Corinthians 5:17; 11:2; Galatians 3:26; Ephesians 5:25-27, 31-32; Colossians 1:19-23; 1 Peter 2:9-10; 1 John 3:1-2; Revelation 19:7-8; 21:2, 9.

[77] While also universal, the local expression of the body of Christ takes on very specific features as a unique work of God in a specific place and time. Therefore, part of our job as leaders is to explore and discern the context of our community with missiological lenses—going as missionaries to our culture in the same way we would go to a foreign culture. Because of radical shifts in American culture and the lack of the typical American church paying any attention to these shifts, we certainly have work to do in contextualizing our ministries!

DEEP DESIGN PROMPT

History: Our worship needs to acknowledge more of life's disorientation.

The work of theologian Walter Brueggemann can help youth workers who want deeper worship to tap into the context of their students. The Psalms hold a full 65 laments, or "psalms of *disorientation*," as Brueggemann terms them. Yet our corporate worship rarely, if ever, includes lament language. As Brueggemann suggests, "The problem with a hymnody [the collected songs, rituals, and prayers a church uses] that focuses on equilibrium, coherence, and symmetry…is that it may deceive and cover over. Life is not like that. Life is also savagely marked by disequilibrium, incoherence, and unrelieved asymmetry."[78]

DEEP DESIGN PROMPT

Experience: Adolescents connect with suffering during worship.

Youth get this. The pains of loneliness, abandonment, and hopelessness mark their worlds. It could be argued that *disorientation* provides an appropriate label for the adolescent experience. The God who understands suffering appeals to a generation looking for something or someone worthy of suffering for, and who is willing to suffer in love for them.[79]

An identity-attentive worshiping community allows space both for authentic lament and for hope in the midst of suffering. When students deeply grieve the loss of a classmate to cancer, and we give them the chance to speak (or sing, draw, or write out) their pain in worship, we create a community that invites the hard questions. These questions take us to places of doubt before we can return again to places of faith and trust. In essence, the lament makes way for healing.

For more on lament and its place in Scripture and your youth worship, check out www.cyfm.net.

Lament for our students may involve personal or community sin, personal loss, grief on behalf of friends in difficult circumstances, or injustice and pain on a community or world level. How do we help Karl, who associates "parents" primarily with abuse and neglect, worship a God who we claim is the perfect Parent? What about the deep sense of shame and regret Lina feels about her sexual

---

[78] Walter Brueggemann, *The Message of the Psalms: A Theological Commentary*, (Augsburg Old Testament Studies, Minneapolis: Augsburg, 1984), 51.

[79] Kenda Creasy Dean, "Moshing for Jesus: Adolescence as a Cultural Context for Worship," in Tim A. Dearborn & Scott Coil, eds, *Worship at the Next Level: Insight from Contemporary Voices,* (Grand Rapids: BakerBooks, 2004), 125-126.

encounters with several boys over the last year? Will she be able to offer heartfelt praise to God without first lamenting the loss and disappointment she's experienced? Lament, in part, enables Karl, Lina, and the rest of us to hope genuinely.

Dialogue

When it comes to lament and other issues, how will you know if you "get" the context of your students? One easy way to stimulate **New** dialogue is through a survey. Recently I designed a simple survey to collect reflections and observations from students in several churches. The survey invites students to discuss and evaluate the ways their youth ministries and churches worship together. The survey used simple questions, such as:

∞ DEEP DESIGN PROMPT

Experience: One great way to understand your context is through a survey.

For more on how to dialogue with (or survey) your students, see Chapter 12 on focus groups.

- How important to you is being part of a group of people who regularly worship God together?

- What have you grown to understand about yourself, others, your church, and God through worshiping with others?

- *Why* do you worship with others?

After taking this survey, one student brought up the question of whether worship is primarily individual or corporate. She insisted that worshiping God is a solitary experience, and the people around us "just happen to be there" as we worship (an attitude reflected in several responses). So then the conversation shifted to other questions such as:

- "What would be missing if you were not part of worship at your church?"

- "Who would care if you didn't show up?"

Over the course of the conversation, several students realized worship may be about more than simply "me and God." Students long to know the answer to that question—*does it matter if I show up?* In this scenario, a survey provided a launching point for deeper learning.

Along with your ministry team, you might want to study your communal worship life—its practices, rituals, and interactions with one another and with God—by asking:

- Are there any fallacies communicated through the way we conduct worship or by the people we exclude from worship?

- Do our services emphasize fragmented families and community, whisking off youth and children to other parts of the church while adults experience "real" worship?

- Do we really believe what we are singing, praying, speaking, and displaying visually in our worship?

Regular dialogue with these kinds of questions allows the ministry team to affirm or adjust areas of ministry as needed, guarding against unhealthy patterns.

Ritual

Rituals are powerful ways of transmitting identity, especially rituals that involve rites of passage in the journey to adulthood.

Liturgy = the "service" of the people, through worship.

Liturgy has generally come to mean the rites, practices, and common worship language of a church. Even the traditional liturgies of the church—which youth pastors tend to dismiss habitually—can help frame adolescent spiritual experiences within a broader and deeper collective identity. Maybe it's time for the youth worker community to revisit the "stuff they do (or used to do) on Sunday morning in 'big church.'"

DEEP MINISTRY

Practicing liturgy invokes *acts of remembrance*, a key theme of the biblical worship narrative. Rites of passage that recall God's activity are important teaching tools in worship that speak a new identity into believers' lives. As Will Willimon notes, "Rites of passage are ritualized journeys across life's most difficult boundaries. They give new meaning to the changes in the status or role of persons, they reestablish equilibrium in persons and communities after the crisis of change, and they…[transmit] to future generations what the community believes to be the meaning of that change."[80]

∞ **DEEP DESIGN PROMPT**

Experience: It's time to revisit the rituals and acts of remembrance we've tended to cast aside.

Baptism is one of the most visual rituals that help us experience our identity as Christians.[81] Baptism offers a response to the "Who am I?" question: "I am the one who is called, washed, named, promised, and commissioned."[82] And this, by necessity, happens in the context of a baptismal community. Those baptized into Christ become inheritors of God's promises and living symbols of the new creation.[83]

∞ **DEEP DESIGN PROMPT**

History: Rites of passage give meaning and a sense of history to students today.

Another primary identity-forming ritual of the church is the Lord's Supper. Eating together creates a sense of family, and Jesus' practice of sharing meals with "saints and sinners" unveils the centrality and power of table fellowship for faith communities. Henri Nouwen teaches that our identities in Christ share the nature of the Eucharist: as the Spirit moves in our lives to form us as the *beloved*, we are "taken, blessed, broken, and given," thus reflecting the actions of the Lord's Supper.[84]

∞ **DEEP DESIGN PROMPT**

History: Both baptism and the Lord's Supper are important rituals that help develop students' identities.

Within your own ministry you might want to ask these questions:

- What other rituals and tools of worship effectively communicate and transpose truths about God and humanity into the adolescent reality?

[80] Willimon, *Worship as Pastoral Care*, 102.
[81] Ibid, 148.
[82] Ibid, 154.
[83] Don E. Saliers, *Worship as Theology: Foretaste of Glory Divine* (Nashville: Abingdon, 1994), 59.
[84] Nouwen, *Life of the Beloved*, 48-49.

- How can we create further rituals of table fellowship, incorporating youth into the life of the community?

- How can baptism and/or confirmation rites include significant opportunities for others to confer on them new identities in Christ?

∞ **DEEP DESIGN PROMPT**

Experience: If we don't give kids rituals and initiation rites, they'll create their own cheap imitations.

If the church leaves kids without any initiation rites—if they are left with only our culture's cheap imitations and "graduations"—they will be forced to initiate one another, taking on roles abandoned by appropriate guides. Worship can be either a spawning pool or a cesspool for identity formation, depending in part upon its leadership. What kind of pool are our kids swimming in from week to week at our churches?

Caveats

A few warnings seem appropriate here.

If you want an even deeper understanding of the role of rituals and rites of passage in your youth worship, check out www.cyfm.net.

First, the last thing we want is to make following Jesus more complicated or obscure. "Rites of passage" can sound and feel like fraternity rituals (think *secret handshakes* and *group humiliation*). Following Jesus should never require that. Sacred moments do not have to be complicated to be profound. Actions such as piling rocks together to create a simple altar or laying hands on a young person's head while anointing her with oil create space for a deeply formative interaction with God.

∞ **DEEP DESIGN PROMPT**

Experience: Although glorifying God is the primary purpose of worship, along the way we can pick up valuable lessons about our identity.

Second, self-discovery is never the *point* of our worship. Glorifying God must remain our central focus. Yet as we glorify God, we will inevitably learn about ourselves. The questions then become *what are we learning together as a community?* and *Is what we are learning accurate?* As we ask and answer these questions, far from singing ourselves nowhere, we will see the kingdom of God breaking through in the lives of our churches.

DEEP DESIGN, STEP 3 (OBSERVATION): *WHO?*

Hal Hamilton, pastor to students at Aldersgate United Methodist Church in Marion, Illinois, has been wrestling with questions like these for years. The answers he's discovered (and sometimes stumbled into) can help you and your team consider how your worship can offer deeper meaning and significance.

Hal, you are a professing non-musician. How has this influenced the nature and tone of worship in your student ministry?

Because I'm not a musician, I think it's been easier for me and my students to grasp that worship is more than just singing a few songs. I'm a worship leader, yet I don't play music. Clearly worship is more than music. But when it comes to music, I've had to learn to empower musicians and others in their gifts.

So how do you try to help other non-musicians learn to worship?

One year, as we were developing a new type of worship service, I looked at a specific student who was not a musician. His dad, who had helped lead worship music in another church, had recently walked out on the family. This kid was a computer whiz, so I asked myself, "How do I help him worship?" I approached him and asked if he could build a computer for us to use in worship as his act of worship. He was transformed. He uncovered an identity that benefited our community, partly because his skills shaped our worship in ways that mattered to him and to the community.

How else do you try to involve kids in your worship leading and planning?

One thing we do currently in our community is extend an invitation for all of the worshiping community to come together from 6:30 to 8 on Wednesday nights. This is a time when anybody can bring spiritual gifts. We spend the first 15 minutes talking about the previous service. This is not a negative critique, but a time to ask questions. *Where did we encounter wonder? Where did we encounter transformation? Was the teaching biblical? Was the worship passionate?* Then we start planning for future worship gatherings. As we look at next week's text, we ask who has something to offer—a thought, a gift, whatever. Often the brainstorming with this group is about the look and feel of the worship space—the ambience. There's a lot of ritual in how we decorate our worship space, yet it also shifts based on the text. In some churches the message is, "If you're good enough to sing in the praise band, you're a worshiper, and if you're not, you're not." We're trying to send the message that all of us are worshipers.

How do you think worship impacts students' identity formation?

One of our college interns helped me put into words what happens in worship that shapes our identity. She referred to 1 John 4:18, which says, "Perfect love casts out all fear." When we worship, we encounter the One who is perfect love. As he casts out fear, we're able to become more open, more honest, and more authentic. We're able to understand what it means to be the people God has called us to be.

DEEP MINISTRY

What do you do to understand the particular fears and struggles of students in your context?

This comes not out of the worship service itself, but out of being a community where adults love Jesus passionately and walk alongside students with authenticity and appropriate vulnerability. As we share life together, these things emerge. The students have watched godly adults struggle—with cancer, the failure of a business, prodigal kids, unemployment, surgeries, death of parents, broken living room furniture, and a lot more—with grace and openness. That goes a long way toward opening the door to discovering the fears and struggles of the young people whose lives they have shared.

As someone who has been in youth ministry for 20 years, in what ways has your approach to student worship changed?

I used to be pretty directive in the way I led worship. In college I coordinated weekend worship teams that would visit churches and lead services. I mostly handpicked my teams and told them what to do. I felt there were formulas you could use, with the right people, to obtain the right results. But my philosophy and approach have changed. There's something in me that rises up against technique as the central focus in worship. I don't necessarily want students to have a great youth group experience. If they struggle through youth group but have fruit that lasts, it's worth it. That makes our programming and worship messy—which goes against my personality. But I find myself strangely loving it.

What do you mean by "messy" worship experiences?

I don't mean being thoughtless and just winging it. Instead, I mean valuing empowerment over excellence. I mean promoting process over performance. I mean the freedom to be real as kingdom people who live in the real world with real issues and pain, who are broken and sometimes a mess, but who also worship a real God.

In some youth ministries, worship has become equated with what we do together on Sundays. How do you view worship?

I've been teaching recently on "Eating with Jesus," mostly from Luke. We've found that something powerful happens when we discuss the kingdom of God and interact with the kingdom around the table. We have been encouraging our community to build hospitality throughout the week and gather around tables and wrestle through issues of following Jesus. That helps students think about hospitality as an act of worship that makes us a worshiping community throughout the week, not only when we come together at a worship service.

How do you try to incorporate students into the worship life of the church?

The church is one of the few places in American culture where three, four, and maybe even five generations can still gather together. Yet we usually segregate ourselves in different rooms. At some point I started getting serious about the whole community worshiping together.

When we only let kids express their passion for God when they're performing one Sunday a year on "Youth Sunday," that's not kingdom. If we really believe Jesus' words and his teaching about worship and about community, then we've got to provide opportunities for people of every age to be worshiping. In our church, we integrate teenagers as liturgists, and we encourage students to join the choir because we think intergenerational worship is best for the whole Body.

What role does the ritual of communion play in your worship?

The way we worship together is fairly sacramental. Communion reminds us of our brokenness and allows us to celebrate in the midst of that brokenness. We take communion every week, framing it in the context of the good news. In our community, God's Word always takes us to communion. We do it in different ways, but it's a regular ritual.

What other significant worship rituals are students involved in?

We have a number of rite-of-passage rituals, but most of them are outside the context of corporate worship and more programmatic. One powerful worship ritual we have involves our worship space. We meet in a gym, and setting it up for worship has become a ritual act of worship. There is a buzz and a community happening for an hour before the service that is completely energizing.

Why do you think so many youth ministries don't give time in- their worship for students to experience the type of lament that was experienced by the writers of the Psalms?

I think there are people who are afraid that if they begin to grieve, the black hole would be so huge that it would swallow them. If as the leader I'm not sure I won't get lost in that pit, how in the world am I going to take someone else there?

For youth workers who want to lead their students into more experiences of Psalm-like lament, what would you recommend?

I have to admit, I haven't explored this a great deal yet. It seems to me that studying the psalms of lament together and allowing the students to respond by writing and speaking their own experiences in the form of a psalm of lament might be a good opportunity. Or perhaps discussing movie clips that leave a lack of resolution or a sense of disequilibrium. Or maybe structuring an entire worship gathering around a psalm of lament and allowing students to express their uncertainties in prayer.

Any more suggestions for youth workers who might feel clueless or helpless when it comes to planning and leading worship meaningfully?

The students and adults in your community are exactly who God wants to help lead your worship times. If you don't have the world's best singer or guitar player in your community, you must not need them.

DEEP DESIGN, STEP 4 (APPLICATION): *HOW?*

Application Questions:

∞ DEEP DESIGN
PROMPT

STEP 1: NOW?   STEP 3: WHO?

STEP 4: HOW?   STEP 2: NEW?

1. What do you think your students are learning about God and themselves from your current worship experiences and services? What is good about what they're learning? What do you wish they were learning?

2. If you created a survey about worship for youth in your care, do you expect you might find that your youth have views similar to the youth in this chapter (e.g., that worship is individual, between me and God)? What kinds of questions do you want to ask them now?

3. What rituals do you have that are particularly meaningful in worship? What do you think students are learning about themselves through those rituals? What ideas do you have about other rituals that could help students go deeper in their worship and personal growth?

4. How is your worship ministry similar to what Hal describes? How is it different?

5. Which one of the ideas or practices in this chapter do you think you should reflect on in the next month? What other practical ideas do you have to spur identity transformation through deeper worship in your church or ministry?

How are we going to go deeper in our worship?	Source

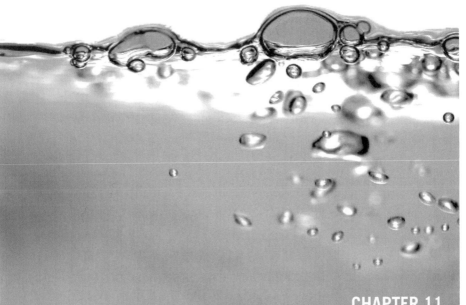

DEEP EXPECTATIONS: WHY AM I EXHAUSTED SO MUCH OF THE TIME, AND WHAT CAN I DO ABOUT IT?

Kara Powell

DEEP DESIGN, STEP 1 (DISCERNMENT): *NOW?*

I love football. My idea of a perfect Sunday is coming home from our church service, making waffles and playing with my kids, turning on a football game, and falling asleep on the couch during halftime. The best Sundays are when one of my two favorite teams is playing on television: the San Diego Chargers—and whoever is playing the Oakland Raiders. Believe it or not, during those Sundays my husband refers to himself as a "football widower."

I've loved football for as long as I can remember. When I was 12, my brother, two neighbor kids, and I formed "A.F.A.S."—or "Alley Football All-Stars." (I don't think we ever trademarked the name, so feel free to use it!) We had plays, we practiced, we had cheers, and when it came to game time, we scored touchdown after touchdown against the other kids in the neighborhood. That is, until mom called us in for dinner.

But even when none of my teammates were around, I still loved to play. I'd hike the ball to myself, take a few steps back, throw the football high into the air, catch it, dodge imaginary defenders, and run as fast as I could for the crack in the sidewalk that marked the end zone. I was a "one woman team." And I played with gusto.[85]

Whether you like football or not, too many youth workers **Now** end up like I ended up in the alley—as one-person teams. Demoralized by a lack of volunteers, frustrated when others let us down, and pressured by others' expectations, we end up shouldering almost total responsibility and control over our ministry.

We end up as Superpastors.

I coined the term *Superpastor* when I was writing my Ph.D. dissertation. To me it represented the best label for what I struggled with, and what I was reading about in

---

[85] Adapted from Kara Eckmann Powell, "Focusing Youth Ministry Through Innovation," in *Starting Right: Thinking Theologically About Youth Ministry*, edited by Kenda Creasy Dean, Chap Clark, and Dave Rahn (Grand Rapids, Michigan: Zondervan Publishing, 2001).

the literature. It's our tendency to believe that, as leaders, we are somehow more than human. We might not believe we're literally "faster than a speeding bullet" or "more powerful than a locomotive," but we start thinking we don't have weaknesses and struggles—or if we do, we'd better not show them to others. When the rest of the world needs to slow down and take a break, we keep going, and going, and going. It's workaholism (or at least hard work on steroids) cloaked in "dedication to God and ministry."

If you've been in ministry long, you've probably experienced some stress and burnout. As part of my Ph.D. research, I compared the stress and burnout rates of pastors with those of people in other caregiving professions (e.g., therapists, doctors, nurses, social workers). To my surprise, pastors' stress and burnout rates are about the same as those other professions.[86]

That means that while we in ministry may be tired, it's not just because of stress or burnout. There has to be something more causing our fatigue. So I started researching an even deeper question: *if it's not just stress and burnout that makes us so tired, what is it?*

After reviewing the research on pastors and Christian leaders, I think I've pinpointed at least part of the answer. While stress and burnout rates are the same for pastors and those in other caregiving professions, there are three clusters of expectations for pastors **Now** that are different than most other jobs.

1. We can do it all.

2. We are the perfect examples.

3. We are always happy.

 **DEEP DESIGN PROMPT**

Hindering God's transformation: We think we're Superpastors.

 **DEEP DESIGN PROMPT**

Creating space for God's transformation: We are willing to work hard.

[86] Kara Eckmann Powell, *Expected Vocational Roles in the Pastorate: An Empirical Examination and a Practical Theology Intervention* (Unpublished dissertation, Fuller Theological Seminary, 2000), 61-63.

Mix these together and get that red cape ready because you've just followed the recipe for the Superpastor Syndrome.

Leaders and youth workers with Superpastor tendencies often feel the following:

DEEP DESIGN PROMPT

Hindering God's transformation: Rest is taboo.

DEEP DESIGN PROMPT

Hindering God's transformation: Comparison and jealousy.

DEEP DESIGN PROMPT

Hindering God's transformation: You focus on criticism.

DEEP DESIGN PROMPT

Hindering God's transformation: People don't know the real you.

DEEP DESIGN PROMPT

Hindering God's transformation: High expectations for others.

- **You can't rest (or at least you're very bad at resting).** You bring work with you on vacation, and you feel guilty when you're home with a cold instead of out with students and leaders.

- **You want to be the best, and you're jealous of others.** While you want others to succeed *somewhat*, you don't want them to succeed more than you.

- **You take a while to shake off criticism.** If others praise most of your ministry and criticize one area, that area becomes like a stain on a white wall. When you look in that direction, all you see is the stain.

- **You have few real friends, especially in your ministry.** That's not to say you don't have meaningful conversations with others; it's just that they're calculated and guarded. As Eugene Peterson confesses about his former congregation, "They make me into a kind of holy persona and expect me to be that for them. It's easy to let them; I like it. And because intimacy is difficult for me, as it is for them, it's more comfortable for me to let that distance develop."[87]

- **You place pressure on your spouse and kids.** You want a high-achieving, well-behaved family, especially when others are looking.

It's unclear whether the sources of these pressures are external (i.e., based on what others expect of us) or internal (i.e., based on what we expect of ourselves). My hunch is that it's a mixture of the two. Regardless of the

---

[87] Eugene Peterson, as quoted in "Leadership Forum: How Pure Must a Pastor Be?" *Leadership Journal*, Spring 1988: 12-20.

sources of the pressure, the result is the same: busyness and fatigue.

How many of us Superpastors are out there? While it's difficult to know for sure, I'd estimate that more than 70 percent of youth workers are Superpastors. (And that's conservative—the real number is probably higher.) For those of you you who aren't math whizzes, that leaves 30 percent who are not Superpastors. At least there are some youth pastors who have found that elusive escape from the Superpastor Syndrome, but how? We'll turn to that now.

> ∞ **DEEP DESIGN PROMPT**
>
> Creating space for God's transformation: There is an escape from the Superpastor Syndrome.

DEEP DESIGN, STEP 2 (REFLECTION): *NEW?*

In the midst of my research about Superpastors, I attended an annual forum hosted by the National Network of Youth Ministries. The first night of the talk, Louie Giglio, leader of the Passion conferences and worship gatherings, presented some **New** perspectives on deep ministry that Superpastors often ignore.

> ∞ **DEEP DESIGN PROMPT**
>
> STEP 1: NOW?   STEP 3: WHO?
>
>
>
> STEP 4: HOW?   **STEP 2: NEW?**

Louie started by talking about the God who is the great I AM—the God who, in the midst of Moses' fear about approaching the people of Israel, promises that "I AM who I am" (Exodus 3:14a). Louie then asked a question I will never forget: "If God is the great I AM, what does that make us?"

> ∞ **DEEP DESIGN PROMPT**
>
> Scripture: God is the great I AM.

Louie paused and then answered his own question, "That makes us the great I AM NOT."

Think about what it means to be the great I AM NOT in youth ministry.

> ∞ **DEEP DESIGN PROMPT**
>
> Scripture: We are the great I AM NOT.

I am not the students' rescuer. God is.

I am not their healer. God is.

I am not their comforter. God is, through his Holy Spirit.

I am not their hope. I am not their peace. I am not their life. God is. God is. God is.

And ultimately, I am not their pastor. God is the ultimate shepherd.

When I speak to groups of pastors and youth workers, I like to say to them, "True or false, you need God." Most agree, "True."

So I continue, "True or false, God needs you."

The quick, knee-jerk reaction for over three-fourths of youth workers I've asked is similarly, "True."

But wait. *Really*? Does the God of the universe need you, oh youth worker, to accomplish his work? Can't he accomplish his work with limestone, elm trees, dandelions, and zebras if he chooses to? Are you really that indispensable? God's definition of himself as I AM tells us he does not *need* us. It's time to reclaim our I AM NOT-ness! It's time to put away the red cape of the Superpastor and put on a T-shirt that says I AM NOT.

∞ DEEP DESIGN PROMPT

Research: Past solutions have encouraged doing "more" of something.

During my research I realized that many efforts to eliminate leaders' fatigue tend to rely on "more" techniques. (This is similar to the "more of the same" solution we discussed in Chapter 1). Exercise more. Sleep more. Eat better. Get into a support group. None of these "solutions" are inherently bad. In fact, most are very helpful. The problem is that they're too shallow. You can do them and still be a Superpastor. In fact, they can even make things worse—becoming another part of the Superpastor lifestyle. To escape the exhausting Superpastor lifestyle and truly live as I AM NOT, we need to stop in our tracks and do a theological U-turn. And that means confronting what I call the "Omni-Temptations."

Omni-Temptation 1: Omnipresence

The first **New** way to live as I AM NOT is to stop pretending you're *omnipresent*. "Omni" means "all," and it's common for youth workers to communicate that we can be everywhere at all times. It sounds pretty silly when you think about it. Only God is present everywhere at all times. But faced with the almost infinite demands of students and families, it's tempting to act like we can be there for them 24/7.

∞ DEEP DESIGN PROMPT

Scripture: Only God is omnipresent.

"Sure, I can make it to the campus Bible study tomorrow. You need me to speak there, too? Yeah, I can do that."

"You want to meet for coffee tomorrow because you're interested in helping lead worship music? Hey, we're desperate for new leaders. Name the time and the place, and I'll be there."

A sophomore named Jennifer taught me that I couldn't be omnipresent—and that this is okay. She walked up to me after church one Sunday and handed me an invitation to her play on Thursday night. "Kara, I'd really like it if you could come see me in the play on Thursday."

I knew I was free Thursday night. I had intentionally kept it open. I was busy Monday, Tuesday, and Wednesday nights, so I wanted to just relax on Thursday.

I had a decision to make. Would I do what she was asking, or would I tell her the truth about my need for rest?

I paused and made my choice. "Jennifer, I'd love to be there on Thursday. I'm really proud of you and am sure you'll do a great job. Technically, I'm free, but I'm out every other night this week with kids or leaders, and really feel like I need to keep that night free to rest."

In the last several years I've decided to honor a weekly commitment to a Sabbath. Having a weekly time to PRAY and PLAY has been one of the most powerful ways I've admitted to myself and to others that I'm not a Superpastor. For more about what Scripture teaches about Sabbath and how you can incorporate it into your life, see our free resources at www.cyfm.net.

Jennifer looked at me and shrugged. "That's okay. I'm glad you're getting the rest you need."

As Jennifer walked away, I was stunned. I just said I couldn't be there for her, and nothing terrible happened! She didn't faint. The earth didn't open up and swallow her—or me. In fact, something very good came of it. She realized I am human—like her—and I needed rest. When Jennifer graduates from high school and looks back on our relationship, I'd rather have her remember me as a balanced person who modeled peace and gentle strength than a shallow youth worker who was always "there for her"—and always exhausted.

Omni-Temptation 2: Omniscience

In addition to realizing you're not omnipresent, living as I AM NOT also means recognizing you're not omniscient. While I may wish I were *omniscient*—or all-knowing—the facts are facts: the amount I don't know about life, God, and people far exceeds what I do know. Instead of admitting they don't have all the answers, Superpastors try to hide their limited knowledge. Instead of resting in life's inevitable ambiguities and channeling energy toward true relationships, Superpastors devote energy toward pretending they don't struggle or doubt

It was another sophomore girl who taught me this lesson. Corrina's grandmother had been diagnosed with cancer the week before summer camp. When we talked about Corrina's grandmother at cabin time, I tried to tell her the Typical Christian Youth Worker Stuff: "Nothing is impossible for God. He can heal her, so let's pray for healing and his will to be done."

During the middle of camp, I got a phone call from home with my own set of bad news. My stepmom had also been diagnosed with cancer, and it had spread to her

lymph nodes. As I ended the phone call, I knew I needed to talk with Corrina. I found her in our cabin with a few other girls and told them my news. I couldn't even finish telling them before I started to weep.

Corrina grabbed me and held on. She started weeping also, and in typical Girls' Cabin at Camp fashion, soon all of us were crying. This time I decided not to pretend I had any answers—for me or Corrina or any of the girls who were going through trauma. When we prayed, it was heartfelt prayer. I confessed to God that I didn't understand cancer, I was frustrated that it had invaded my family, and I wondered aloud if he'd choose to heal my stepmom. Corrina did the same with her grandmother. Other girls did the same with the difficulties they were experiencing.

∞ DEEP DESIGN PROMPT
Experience: It's okay to admit doubt and pain.

Both Corrina's grandmother and my stepmom ended up healed—by God, by the chemotherapy, or by a combination of the two. For that I am most grateful. But I'm also grateful for the **New** depth I learned that week at camp. I don't have to pretend I have the answers. Life is too complex and too gray for my simple solutions.

Omni-Temptation 3: Omnigiftedness

Finally, stepping out of the exhausting Superpastor Syndrome means realizing we are not *omnigifted*. Unfortunately, the gifts and abilities pastors are expected to master have increased exponentially over the last few centuries. H. Newton Malony and Richard I. Hunt have suggested that, even as past images of leadership fade away, the pastor is still expected to play the hero of yesterday while also modeling today's brand of heroism. In the period after the American Civil War, the ideal hero and pastor was a person "of power" whose preaching was forceful and influential over groups and crowds. Toward the end of the 1800s, the new hero became the "lib-

eral progressive"—a pastor who could not only preach powerfully but also pursue social justice and be active in politics, union movements, and slum clearance. Following World War I, a new hero emerged: the competent manager. At this point, pastors were expected to be efficient administrators in addition to passionate preachers and social justice crusaders.[88] While Malony and Hunt stop their analysis at this point, the new approaches to worship and technology that mark the start of the 21st century demand liturgical creativity and computer mastery in addition to all previous job requirements.

∞ DEEP DESIGN PROMPT

History: Expectations have grown for pastors and leaders over recent decades.

Translating that into youth ministry means that youth workers today are generally expected to have...

- The entrepreneurial vision of Bill Gates

- The organizational abilities of Stephen Covey

- The passion of Maya Angelou

- The humor of Jon Stewart

- The counseling skills of Dr. Phil

- The authenticity of Oprah Winfrey

∞ DEEP DESIGN PROMPT

Scripture: God wants me to use my gifts, not yours.

I'll state the obvious: Oprah is Oprah, you are you, and I am me. And God has given each member of the body of Christ unique gifts that he wants us to use. All God expects of me is to use *my* gifts—not *my* gifts plus *your* gifts. So if we're going to escape the tiring expectations of being omni-gifted and instead simply be *me*-gifted, we must step off the Superpastor pedestal and develop a deeper team.

---

[88] H. Newton Malony and Richard A. Hunt, *The Psychology of Clergy* (Harrisburg, PA: Morehouse, 1991), 3, 4.

DEEP DESIGN, STEP 3 (OBSERVATION): *WHO?*

Chris Brooks, president of Urban Reclaim Youth Ministry Foundation in the Twin Cities, is someone **Who** has learned to step off the Superpastor pedestal the hard way. During his 11 years of youth ministry experience in church and parachurch ministries, he has faced plenty of internal and external Superpastor pressures. Only when he "fell flat on his face" did he take off his cape and develop an effective and deep ministry. In his current role of "equipping urban youth workers in Minneapolis and St. Paul with the tools and capacities necessary to fulfill God's call with excellence," he hopes to help others learn from his experience as he continues to learn from theirs.

Chris, you say that when you tried to be a Superpastor, you ended up falling flat on your face. What happened?

In youth ministry, we are often expected to be "one man" or "one woman" shows. When I was serving at my last two churches, I was expected to be the administrator, program implementer, volunteer recruiter and trainer, preacher, and vision caster. To be honest, wearing all those hats made me feel pretty good. People looked up to me because I had all of those responsibilities.

The downside was that I couldn't deliver what was expected of me because I was trying to do too much. Most of what I did, I did really poorly.

Were there any particular areas that suffered?

Definitely teaching. There were times when I was teaching a certain subject, but I didn't know the first thing about it. I'd fool some of the kids and

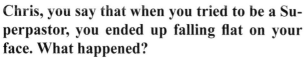

leaders in our group. But people started to catch on that I wasn't teaching any substance. People who knew their stuff started asking, "For real? That's all you've got?"

What did you do as your ministry started to crumble and people started to grumble?

It's always a challenge when you think you're Michael Jordan, and you realize you're a rookie. I had to face the reality that I was in a leadership position I wasn't qualified for, and I was in over my head.

The first thing I did was identify my allies. Stepping out of the Superpastor Syndrome meant some people were going to turn against me. I knew I needed people who would stick with me and support me. I started with my two friends in my accountability group. I met with them, emotionally barfed on the table, and asked them to help me clean it up. I told them I couldn't live like this anymore. Not only was I struggling in my church, but also my wife wasn't pleased and my own kids were getting my leftovers.

Shouldn't your accountability partners have talked with you about this before you hit such a big wall?

They tried, but I wasn't ready. They had tried to help me before with managing my schedule and getting more time with my family, but I didn't really hear them.

What did your two friends do to help you?

I asked them to help me strategize whom I need- ed to talk to, when I should talk to them, what I

should say, and maybe most importantly, what I *shouldn't* say. They encouraged me to go first to a few key stakeholders in our church, like the chair of the board, and ask them to help me work with the men's and women's ministries in our church to mobilize more mentors and teachers.

What about the kids and leaders in your own ministry?

I talked with them after I talked to the church leaders. I put the adult leaders on notice that I was thinking about changing my leadership style, and I wanted them to be praying.

I told the students about my change of heart in a sermon. I'll never forget that day. I confessed to the students that I had focused more on their behavior than on their hearts. I repented and asked for their forgiveness.

The amazing thing is that students not only forgave me but decided to be part of the solution. They met together and asked themselves, "How are we going to help Chris?" Their answer took the form of a new student leadership team. But it was only when I stopped being a Superpastor that we finally had indigenous leadership development.

What types of changes did you make with your adult team?

I totally changed the way we invited and interacted with new leaders. As new leaders came into the group, we started doing a front-end assessment of their gifts, temperaments, and love languages. I wanted to gather as much data as possible about them so they could operate in the areas of their spiritual gifts and strengths. That way they'd not only be more effective, but also they'd stick with us (and their kids) longer.

What instruments or tools were especially helpful in trying to get to know your leaders?

I'm a big fan of the "Strengths Finder" instrument. (See http://www.strengthsquest.com for more information.) I also like the book *Life Keys* by Kise, Stark, and Hirsh because it's very holistic. Another important resource was *Love Languages*, which has helped me figure out what types of affirmation are meaningful to myself and to others (e.g., Words of Affirmation, Physical Touch, Quality Time, Acts of Services, or Gifts).

What changed in the way you trained and nurtured your leaders?

This may sound simplistic, but once we knew how every individual leader wanted to be cared for, it was much easier to care for each person. If someone's love language were quality time, I'd have coffee with them. If they find being encouraged meaningful, I'd try to encourage them either in person or in a note.

Once I realized I couldn't be a Superpastor, I realized I needed other adults to help me nurture these leaders. We invited seasoned adults in our churches to be "coaches" and meet with our adult leaders to talk about their relationships with God and their lives outside of the ministry.

Mark Maines is another youth worker trying to figure out how to escape the Superpastor Syndrome and better coach his leaders. At the end of this chapter, you can find a Coaching Worksheet with questions he asks his leaders. Blank copies of his Coaching Worksheet, as well as a Leadership Assessment Form and related article, can be downloaded for free at www.cyfm.net.

DEEP MINISTRY

Another struggle for Superpastors is finding rest. What did rest look like when you were a Superpastor?

Rest meant nothing to me when I was a Superpastor. There was no concept of rest in my life. Even when I was on vacation, I was thinking about the ministry and calling in daily to make sure everything was okay.

What are you doing differently to rest now?

Now that I'm trying to build the capacity of others, I have great rest. One of my old senior pastors had a motto: "Divert daily, withdraw weekly, and abandon annually." I'm trying to follow that.

Sounds catchy, but what does it mean?

"Divert daily" means that I stop every day and do something unrelated to my ministry work. If I'm 15 minutes early somewhere, I stop by a creek and sit for 10 minutes. I try to keep a worship CD with me so that if I have a few minutes before a meeting, I can listen to some music and connect with God.

"Withdraw weekly" means having a spiritual retreat once a week. To be honest, I don't do it weekly. I do it monthly. But it's a nonnegotiable for me, and it's even in my job description. I block out the whole day and don't make any appointments or take any phone calls. I try to allow God to set the agenda. Sometimes I sense that God wants me to drive through a certain part of town and pray for the people. Some days I go and sit at the basilica or in a church sanctuary and pray for hours. Some days I dig into a spiritual formation book and write in my journal.

"Abandon annually" means taking your darned vacation! Don't save it up, don't bank it. Take it. No wonder our own kids don't think life is very fun when we never get away with them. Saving vacation time is like the Israelites who tried to store up manna. It ends up rotten. When it comes to vacation, use it now, while you've got it.

Are there particular times when you are still tempted to tie on that cape and try to be the superhuman leader?

Unfortunately, I still find myself slipping into Superpastor Syndrome when I feel like I have too much to do and not enough time to delegate. I wish I would slow down, analyze the problem that faces me, and then involve others in solving it. But far too often I either hog the ball or fumble it. I'm still learning to be a team player.

Chris, what advice would you give those who're tired of being Superpastors but are afraid of what others will think if they slow down and become less of a "one person show"?

We'll never be able to end the Superpastor Syndrome on a deep level if we keep perpetuating models of leadership that revolve around one supposedly omnigifted leader. In order to do the great amount of work that needs to be done, we have to empower others.

DEEP DESIGN, STEP 4 (APPLICATION): *HOW?*

Application Questions:

∞ DEEP DESIGN PROMPT

STEP 1: NOW?   STEP 3: WHO?

STEP 4: HOW?   STEP 2: NEW?

1. If you were on trial and accused of being a Super-pastor, what evidence would people use against you? Do you think you'd be convicted?

2. How do you feel when you think about the fact that God is the great "I AM," and you're the great "I AM NOT"?

3. Which of the "omnis" is the greatest temptation for you: feeling like you have to be omniscient, omni-present, or omnigifted? Why do you think that is?

4. How are your ministry and situation similar to Chris's? How are they different?

5. Chris mentioned the effect the Superpastor Syndrome was having on his family. How is your family affected by the way you fall into the Superpastor trap?

6. Chris started by talking with the key stakeholders in his church about involving more people in leadership. Who might you need to talk with in your church about your leadership needs?

7. As Chris talked about the recruiting, training, and nurturing he provides for his staff, what ideas did you get about your own ministry team?

8. As you think about stepping out of the Superpastor Syndrome, how do you think your life or your ministry needs to change so you can go deeper?

How will I go deeper in ministry by stepping out of the Superpastor Syndrome?	Source

COACHING WORKSHEET

	What is going well in our ministry?	What needs to be addressed?	How would you coach me for the future?	Next Steps
Robyn	• Students are enjoying themselves and building community. • Our teaching is becoming a strength. • Our culture is drastically different than one year ago.	• There are various levels of commitment amongst our staff. • Life Group development needs to be developed for leaders. • We need more staff.	• Ask current staff to help recruit new staff. • Invite students to suggest names of adults who seem to care about them and see if any of them want to join our staff.	• Communicate expectations to all staff and ensure commitment. • Develop plan to recruit more adult leaders.
Amy	• Teaching is solid. • Reel Spirituality is great. • Change is gradual but healthy change is occurring.	• We need to adjust our calendar to major holidays (i.e., cancel more Sundays).	• Get input from parents about adjusting the holiday schedule.	• Adjust calendar to include major holidays off; run schedule by a few parents.
Hany	• Consistency has been our strength. • We are regaining students' trust. • There is a growing excitement for the upcoming programs.	• Small groups continue to need development.	• Continue to work hard to connect personally with students. • I think you are doing a great job.	• Continue to recruit, train, and release adult small group leaders.
Billy	• I feel supported and resourced. • I enjoy the freedom to risk and fail. • I gain beneficial perspective from our relationship.	• I need more specific training and development.	• Junior High Leaders desire more personal contact. • Occasional presence in Junior High would be appreciated.	• Create coaching plan that includes specifics and strategies. - philosophy - systems management - advanced planning - adolescent issues

Thanks to Mark Maines for allowing us to include his Coaching Worksheet. Blank copies are available for downloading for free at www.cyfm.net.

CHAPTER 12

DEEP FOCUS GROUPS: IN THE MIDST OF BUSYNESS AND CRAZY EXPECTATIONS, HOW CAN WE MAINTAIN DEEP MINISTRY?

Kara Powell

DEEP DESIGN, STEP 1 (DISCERNMENT): *NOW?*

> "We are half-hearted creatures...[Each of us is] like an ignorant child who wants to go on making mud pies in a slum because he cannot imagine what is meant by the offer of a holiday at the sea. We are far too easily pleased."[89]
>
> —C. S. LEWIS

∞ DEEP DESIGN PROMPT

Hindering God's transformation: We often play in the mud instead of spending time at sea.

Although it's been decades since C.S. Lewis wrote about the vivid differences between the promises of the gospel and our own desires, his words ring true for youth workers today. For a time, a little water and a lot of dirt add up to messy fun. If we're lucky, we might even find a few others whose simple tastes draw them to play with us.

But it's only a matter of time (like about two minutes) before we realize that mud pies aren't all that appetizing. Those who've been playing with us walk off, hoping to find more enticing entertainment. We end up alone with nothing but a soggy mess.

Hopefully this book has helped us learn that the good news—scratch that, the GREAT news—is that God offers us more.

Much, much more.

∞ DEEP DESIGN PROMPT

Creating space for God's transformation: Offering us more than we ever dreamed.

He offers us a holiday at sea. He invites us to relish life's bright sunlight and cool breezes. He beckons us to wiggle our toes in the sand and then swim into the deep, refreshing waters.

At this point in the book, maybe you're excited about deep ministry, but you're also scared it won't last. You're

---

[89] C.S. Lewis, *The Weight of Glory and Other Addresses*, rev. ed. New York: Macmillan, 1980 (orig. 1949), 3-4.

worried that the busyness of life and ministry will keep you digging in the mud instead of racing through the waves.

The question is: *what is it that will keep us from living and ministering with the same metaphorical mud in the same allegorical slum? What will keep us from returning to the shallow ways of youth ministry as we've always done ivt?*

In the quote opening this chapter, Lewis gives one possible answer.

Imagine.

Good ol' Clive was right. One major difference between a shallow life and a deep life is the appreciation we have for what it means to follow God in new and fresh ways.

Imagination and *newness* are imbedded in the Deep Design process. As we've noted, our Deep Design is in the shape of the mathematical infinity sign (a.k.a., a sideways figure "8").

STEP 1: NOW?   **STEP 3: WHO?**

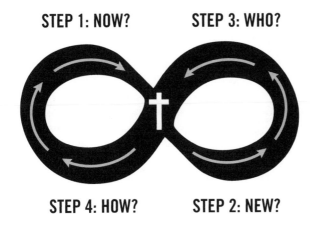

STEP 4: HOW?   **STEP 2: NEW?**

 **DEEP DESIGN PROMPT**

Creating space for God's transformation: Inviting us to an ongoing process of deep ministry.

In research terms, we call this ongoing process a "feedback loop." Every time you figure out **How** to live out deep ministry, you've created a fresh **Now** that you get to explore and evaluate.

We wish it weren't this way, but the reality is that the problems we face **Now** are largely the result of yesterday's solutions. Every time God helps us make some progress toward deep ministry, we'll inevitably stumble upon—and sometimes create ourselves—new dilemmas and challenges. Often the answer to the question, "How did we get here?" is simple: "We brought ourselves here."

This is exactly what happened to Kara:

> I tried to recruit a more diverse adult volunteer team. Realizing I wasn't a Superpastor (see Chapter 11), I assessed our adult volunteers to try to figure out their strengths and weaknesses. Not only did we need more adult leaders, but also we needed younger leaders. We had all sorts of parents involved, but hardly any college students or young adults.

> We prayed. We visited college campuses. We made announcements in the young adult classes at our church. We asked our kids for names of young adults they'd like to spend time with, and then invited those adults to check out our ministry.

∞ DEEP DESIGN PROMPT

Hindering God's transformation: Balance is something we swing through on our way from one extreme to another.

> The good news is that God brought all sorts of dynamic, energetic young leaders to our ministry. The bad news is that a year or so later, we had a new need: we needed some more gray hairs in our leadership.

Balance is something we often swing through on our way from one extreme to another.

So the job of figuring out deep ministry in a shallow world is never done. We can't reach a certain depth and stay there forever. We'll get bored, our programs will get shallow, and our kids will start climbing out of the pool. If we want to maintain the right depth, we have to keep interacting with our kids, families, and community. We have to continue asking the important questions about where we are **Now**, what **New** directions to which we want to head, **Who** has already blazed a trail for us, and **How** we might get there.

DEEP DESIGN, STEP 2 (REFLECTION): *NEW?*

An underlying theme in this book is that the God we serve is creative and keeps involving us in this creative process.

An underlying theme in this *chapter* is that the God we serve is also relational and models what it means to engage in this creative process with others.

In academic circles, there has been a resurgence of interest in the power and connectedness that God models in the Trinity. While the term *Trinity* never appears in Scripture, we can piece together an understanding of the three forms of God through various passages. From the New Testament, we know God is one (Galatians 3:20; James 2:19) but the Son (John 1:1; Colossians 2:9) and the Spirit (Acts 5:3-4) are also fully God.[90]

> **∞ DEEP DESIGN PROMPT**
> Scripture: There are three forms of God.

Though the Son and the Spirit share in the Father's divine nature, they are distinct from the Father. The earliest Christian theologians often thought of the differences in terms of a double movement within God. The first movement is the "generation" that differentiates the Father from the Son, since the Father is the one who generates the Son. The second movement is the "procession" that differentiates the Spirit from the Father and Son, for it is the Spirit

> **∞ DEEP DESIGN PROMPT**
> History: The three forms have distinct roles.

[90] Walter A. Elwell, *Evangelical Dictionary of Theology* (Grand Rapids: Baker Academic, 2001), 502.

who proceeds from both.[91] These two movements are evident in the three distinct actions involved in salvation. The Father plans salvation, the Son provides it, and the Holy Spirit applies it.[92] Similarly, while all are involved in divine revelation through Scripture, it was the Father who had the creative idea for it, the Son who actively expressed it, and the Spirit who illumines it today.[93]

In the early centuries of the church, great debates emerged about the exact nature of the Trinity. Some questioned whether the three forms are "of the same substance" or "of a similar substance." A second controversial issue was whether or not there are actually three forms of God. Some intellectual leaders of the church proposed that the Father, Son, and Holy Spirit are not distinct persons but successive revelations of the same person. In this "modalistic" approach to the Trinity, God was described as one person with three different names and activities.

∞ DEEP DESIGN PROMPT

History: In the fourth century, God was described as "one substance in three modes."

∞ DEEP DESIGN PROMPT

History: The Trinity is a model for what it means to be in partnership.

In the fourth century, leaders gathered at the Council of Constantinople issued a definitive statement addressing both controversies. They described the dynamic relationship among the three forms of God as "one substance in three modes." In this description, the tension between two key facets of the Trinity is maintained—the three forms are *unique* in their roles yet *united* in their divinity and purpose.

In describing the unique but united Trinity, theologian Stanley Grenz writes, "The implications of this conception are immense. Above all, it suggests that God is himself relational. The Father, Son, and Spirit are the social Trinity."[94] Part of what it means for humans to be created in the image of God (in Latin, *imago Dei*), is that we are created with that same sense of relationality. As God interrelates in three complementary persons in divine work, so we humans have the opportunity to relate with others as

[91] Stanley J. Grenz, *Theology for the Community of God* (Michigan: Eerdmans, 1994), 67.
[92] Gordon R. Lewis and Bruce A. Demarest, *Integrative Theology* (Grand Rapids: Zondervan, 1996), 280.
[93] Lewis and Demarest, *Integrative Theology*, 280.
[94] Grenz, *Theology for the Community of God*, 76.

DEEP MINISTRY

we do God's work. As we relate well and deeply with others, we live out God's image in us.

When it comes to youth ministry, following this example means we realize we can't bring about sustainable deep change on our own. As we observe in the Trinity, we reach our deepest potential by functioning as a *united* community with other members who have valuable and *unique* contributions.

There are many ways to engage with others in bringing *ongoing* depth to your ministry. One is to develop the types of teams discussed in Chapters 7 and 11. A second way to draw from the unique perspectives of others is through a research tool that has been hidden and buried for all too long: focus groups. A focus group gathers six to 10 people for a thoughtful conversation about a particular topic. There are many advantages to hosting focus groups: they don't cost much (a box of doughnuts usually does the trick); you can ask follow-up questions to probe beneath the surface of what is being said; and you get results pretty quickly. While focus groups have some limitations (e.g., they're only as good as the questions being asked, the person doing the asking, and the group doing the answering), by following some basic and established focus-group practices, you can get some great **New** data that will help you figure out how to grow deeper.

1. **Figure out the goal and scope of your focus group.** Do you want to assess your entire ministry? Or would you rather focus on a single element of your ministry, such as teaching or mission trips? Is there a program or ministry you're launching soon about which you could use more input? These are all great goals and scopes of focus groups.

2. **Determine who you'll invite.** You can only figure out who you're going to invite once you've com-

∞ **DEEP DESIGN PROMPT**

Research: Focus groups help us figure out what others are thinking.

∞ **DEEP DESIGN PROMPT**

Research: When done well, focus groups get us great information quickly and cheaply.

∞ **DEEP DESIGN PROMPT**

Research: The first step is to figure out the purpose of the focus group.

pleted the first step and know what you're hoping to discover. When our junior high ministry became concerned that our outreach to non-Christian kids was getting shallow, we decided to figure out why by holding two focus groups: one with kids who were committed to our ministry, and another with kids who had been invited by friends. Depending on what you're trying to learn, you might gather a focus group of parents, or kids who have grown estranged from your ministry, or kids who have graduated from your ministry, or adult volunteers, or small group leaders, or youth workers from other churches.

3. **Find one or two facilitators.** You might be a good person to facilitate the group, but you may not be the best person. Students and adults might be hesitant to share if you're in the room, or their sharing might be colored by your presence. You might also end up sounding—or even feeling—defensive in the type and tone of your questions. If possible, try to find somebody who's part insider and part outsider. Maybe it could be a former volunteer, or a parent of kids who've graduated. The ideal is to have someone lead the group who "gets" your group but won't take criticism personally. In general, it's a good idea to find a cofacilitator who can assist the facilitator both by asking questions periodically and more importantly by taking notes about what is being said.

4. **Develop your questions.** Even if you have the right group of people, you won't get much traction if you ask the wrong group of questions. There are several different types of questions you want to try to avoid. First, avoid questions that can be answered with a simple "yes" or "no"—they won't stimulate much conversation. Second, steer clear of leading

questions that might reflect your own opinions (e.g., "What did you think about the great retreat we had last month?"). Third, try to stay away from questions that begin with the word *why*, because it can make some people defensive. (Instead, try asking, "what are some reasons" or another similar phrase.) If you're hosting a 60- to 90-minute focus group with six to 10 people, you probably want to have six to 10 questions prepared.

5. **Have someone review your questions in advance.** Questions and phrases that sound right in your head might sound confusing or jumbled in everyone else's. Ask a trusted colleague or volunteer who will not be part of the focus group to read over the questions in advance.

6. **Choose an appropriate setting and atmosphere.** You want a place that's quiet where you won't be interrupted. (So the youth room might not work so well!) You want people to take their roles seriously, but you also want them to be comfortable— so make sure lighting is adequate and room temperature appropriate. You may also want to bring snacks to help people feel welcome and appreciated (hence, the doughnuts).

7. **Start the meeting well.** Your facilitators should introduce themselves and make sure everyone around the circle introduces himself or herself. It's wise to explain that even though their comments will be shared afterwards, they will be shared anonymously so no one will know who said what—or even who was in the group.

8. **Listen. Listen. Listen. Probe. Probe. Probe.** The facilitator needs to be 100 percent focused on what people are saying. As a listener and facilitator, the

∞ DEEP DESIGN PROMPT

Research: Coming up with the right six to 10 questions is crucial.

∞ DEEP DESIGN PROMPT

Research: Make sure your questions make sense and are clear—to someone other than yourself!

For samples of questions used with an actual youth group, check out the free article entitled "Reading Between the Lines" on the CYFM site at www.cyfm.net.

∞ DEEP DESIGN PROMPT

Research: A good leader will listen and delve deeper.

leader should try not to express undue enthusiasm or disagreement with any comment made, since that will bias the discussion. When appropriate, the facilitator can ask unscripted follow-up questions to delve deeper, clear up confusion, and explore contradictions. It's also the facilitator's job to keep the session focused and steer the conversation back on course as needed.

9. **Process by asking** *What? So what? Now what?* In Chapter 9, we introduced three key questions that could be used in debriefing mission trips: *What? So what? Now what?* The facilitators can use the same questions to debrief the focus group experience after the session has ended and everyone has left. *What* was it that people seemed to be saying? *So what* are some conclusions we can draw for our ministry? *Now what* can we do to implement these changes?

10. **Share the results.** Determine who will most benefit from hearing the results of the focus group. Is it your leadership team? Your students? Their parents? Others in your community? Determine the best time and format to share your results (either through an oral or written report) and discuss what has been discovered.

DEEP DESIGN, STEPS 3 (OBSERVATION) AND 4 (APPLICATION): *WHO* AND *HOW?*

In this final chapter of our book, we decided not to profile any youth workers or share their stories. We've done plenty of that throughout the rest of the book.

It's time for you to be the story. It's time for you to be the youth worker **Who** puts these principles into practice

DEEP DESIGN PROMPT

Research: In addition to data, potential implications and solutions can emerge from your groups as well.

DEEP DESIGN PROMPT

Research: Get the results to the right people at the right time.[95]

DEEP DESIGN PROMPT

STEP 1: NOW?   STEP 3: WHO?

STEP 4: HOW?   STEP 2: NEW?

---

[95] Many of these principles are described more fully in Richard A. Krueger, *Focus Groups* (Thousand Oaks, CA: Sage Publications, 1994) and the *Social Research Update*, no.19, winter 1997, http://www.soc.surrey.ac.uk/sru/SRU19.html.

and lets the Holy Spirit unleash something **New** in your ministry. As you seek God, he will help you come up with fresh ways to develop deep ministry in a shallow world. Committing to ongoing evaluation sends the liberating message to others involved in the ministry that you will never be "perfect" but are on a constant journey of growth and depth.

So grab your towel and get ready for an adventure. It's a wild swim that you've always wanted to try. And now you know **How**.

Application Questions:

1. Do you ever wish you could just figure out the right depth for your ministry, get there, and then stay there until you retire? What is appealing to you about that? What makes that unrealistic?

2. What ministry issues are percolating in your mind that you think could be addressed through focus groups?

3. Whom would you want to invite?

4. Who would be a good facilitator and cofacilitator?

5. What specific questions would you like to ask?

6. How would you like to share the findings and with whom?

7. What makes the Deep Design process a "wild swim"? Are you ready to try it? If not, what obstacles do you still need to overcome? If so, what are some good initial steps?

How am I going to go deeper in my life and ministry...	Source

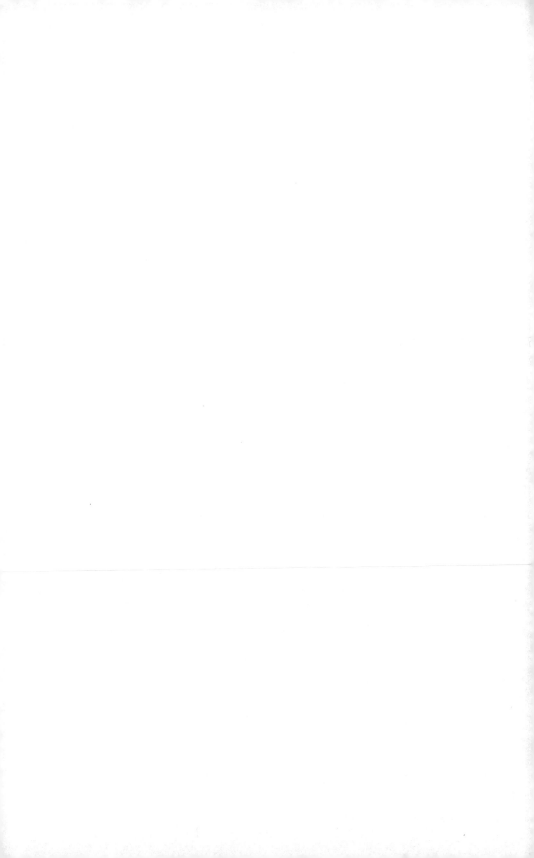

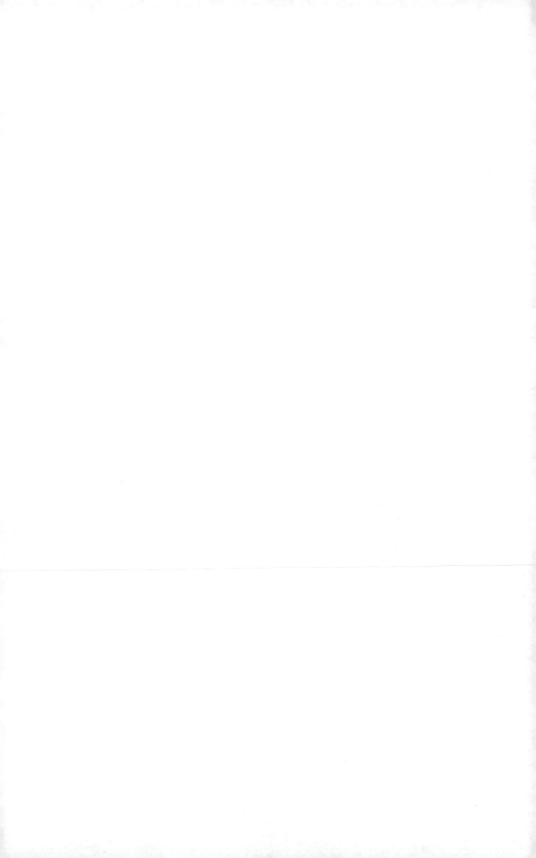